PENGUIN BOOKS

WITNESSES OF REMEMBRANCE

Kunwar Narain (1927–2017) is considered one of India's foremost poets, thinkers and literary figures of modern times. He read widely across disciplines, languages and literatures, and blended an international sensibility with a grounding in Indian history and thought. His diverse oeuvre of seven decades includes three epical poems, eight poetry collections, translations of world poetry, and books of short stories, literary criticism, essays, diaries, conversations, and writings on world cinema and the arts—embodying, above all, a unique interplay of the simple and the complex. His honours include the Sahitya Akademi Award and its Senior Fellowship, the Kabir Samman, medal of Warsaw University, Italy's Premio Feronia for distinguished world author, the Padma Bhushan and the Jnanpith Award. Some of his works still remain unpublished.

Apurva Narain is Kunwar Narain's son and translator. His books of translation include the poetry collection, *No Other World*, and a co-translated collection of short stories, *The Play of Dolls*. His work has appeared in several literary journals over the years. Educated in India and at the University of Cambridge, he writes in English. He also has professional interests in the fields of international development, public health, ethics and ecology.

witnesses of remembrance

selected newer poems

Kunwar Narain

translated by
Apurva Narain

PENGUIN BOOKS

An imprint of Penguin Random House

PENGUIN BOOKS

USA | Canada | UK | Ireland | Australia
New Zealand | India | South Africa | China | Singapore

Penguin Books is part of the Penguin Random House group of companies
whose addresses can be found at global.penguinrandomhouse.com

Published by Penguin Random House India Pvt. Ltd
4th Floor, Capital Tower 1, MG Road,
Gurugram 122 002, Haryana, India

Penguin
Random House
India

First published by Eka, an imprint of Westland Publications Pvt Ltd 2021
Published in Penguin Books by Penguin Random House India 2024

Text and Image Copyright © Apurva Narain 2021

Images in the section breaks are of Kunwar Narain's personal belongings.
Manuscripts, and the doodle with 'The Half a Minute Dream', are from his
notebooks. The sculpture shown with 'A World Under My Feet' is by Siraj
Saxena, the sketch with 'Contemplating a Sketch of Me Made by a Chinese
Poet-Friend' is by Yang Lian, and the sculpture shown with 'Some Days in
Another Time, Another Place' is by Pankaj Agrawal.

ISBN 9780143464082

Typeset in Adobe Caslon Pro by Manipal Technologies Limited, Manipal

Printed at Repro India Limited

www.penguin.co.in

MIX
Paper from
responsible sources
FSC® C047271

For my parents

Contents

Introduction

I remember a river flowing inside my father and never growing old; a whole forest of intimate, detached trees, birds, people, stones and reveries evolving all around it; and the dark cosmic sea of a world hardly yet begun, in which we immersed. I remember the silent history of words; the mirrors and places that all of us lived in unreal time; and the dizzying constellation of memories and wishes and stars through which we tried to map our journeys and our meditations. I remember the circles of chance and choice that he, she, we, all of us, circussed through in the carnival; and the curious colours of cities through which nomads, kings and ordinary human beings loved, wept and passed.

Even as these random allusions to my father's creation of a poetic world flit through my mind, I look back and see that these may not be as random as they seem after all. Even as I engage with his poems one by one, as they dawn on me each day, I find that the whole is far more than the sum of its parts... that they may be connected to much more than meets the eye. And even as I recall his inability to deal with the world on worldly terms—my world or his, your world or ours—to the limit of being aloof, impractical, even other-worldly, do I realise that Kunwar Narain's other-worldliness—an 'inner sight' that sees beyond the eye—has in fact been a most caring, practical and sane voice to save this same world of ours. For as one looks back at how extreme the world has become—from despotic regimes and violent societies, to ecological crises and apocalyptic pandemics, to the apogees of commercialism and consumerism that we have become, to injustice, anxiety and othering at every level—it's our worldly ways that, for Narain, often diminish our world. His loving, gentle and graceful ways out of this—not just in a metaphysical or spiritual sense but also in the life lived and the word written; in the humility and honesty of humdrum, anonymous life—are what these poems have intimately witnessed. They have lived his life as much as their own life and afterlife. Mixed with their remembrances are the poet's memories of his world, my memories of him and, dare I say, perhaps some of your memories of your worlds. For what begins as a personal response to internalised experience can beget much more; experiences worth remembering, in a sense, include the experiences of others.

At varying points in Narain's work, dream and reality, self and other, past and future, hope and dejection, time and place, tree and person, love and art, life and death… intermix. His vision allows for the oneness of things, animate and inanimate. The poems speak of innocence and the loss of innocence, of creation and the cosmos, of lost worlds and exile, of the futility of ambition, haste and achievement. Their technique is eclectic and egalitarian, speaking a truth that can ultimately only be the truth of paradox. At times they speak in a voice that some philosophers have sought, in literature rather than in academia. Others have a zen-like purity. Some are reminiscent of poets like Quasimodo, Jacottet, Carlos Williams or the later Borges in their relative directness. Some are thought-centric, almost scientific, in temperament. The poet feels intensely, thinks intensely; and if the expression of this at times entails a composite simplicity, stillness, even silence, maybe it is because he is also intensely honest; as if any prowess or artifice would go against a truly intimate conversation with himself and his reader.

*

Poetry for Narain has been a way of life, a way to the inner sanctum of wonder and peace that literature and the arts were meant to cultivate. The poems can be a memory, a comment, a discovery, all at once. In this sense, they often have an autobiographical or (a post-postmodern) autofictional element, and ultimately a vision of the self, which seeks to embrace the outer world and then merge with it into an entirety, a universal self, where no one is 'the other' and there is 'no other world'.[1] Poetry is also often a medium of discovery for him, almost in a way science is—and, for instance, in a way Kafka's *Metamorphosis* is a consummate discovery of what human change could be all about.

In his persona and poetry, there is something serene, noble, even fragile, opening itself up to all… Buddha and Gandhi come to his poems, as do the counter-instances of a Nero or a Pol Pot. Federico García Lorca said, '*The artist, and particularly the poet, is always an anarchist in the best sense of the word. He must heed only the call that arises within him from three strong voices: the voice of death, with all its foreboding, the voice of love, and the voice of art.*'[2] These are also the voices that call Narain. His 'anarchy' is his own unremitting sense of purity, peace and love—lived and written—at a time when these words are leaving us, when '… *perhaps they turn into hermits / or seclude themselves so far away / that no language is able / to reach them again.*'[3]

---

[1] Kunwar Narain, *No Other World: Selected Poems*, trans. Apurva Narain, Rupa Publications, India, 2008, & Arc Publications, UK, 2010
[2] Leslie Stainton, *Lorca: A Dream of Life*, Farrar, Straus and Giroux, USA, 1998
[3] From the poem 'Words that Disappear'

Narain has been a reclusive, but engaged, poet for whom writing is like loving or praying, a personal act. In his entire literary journey of seven decades, he never launched his books, went to less than a dozen festivals, and remained reluctant about events, committees and positions of power—a fast-dwindling class in this time of performances and networks. As younger poet Geet Chaturvedi writes of him, '...*He's a sage. He's a saint. He's a poet. It's not just me but a lot of people who use words like these for Kunwar Narain. And this is not a description of some poet from an ancient or medieval age, but of a contemporary poet right here from our times, in the twentieth and twenty-first century... At a time when it is becoming difficult to remember people with the complete, positive intents of these words, when there is a scramble all around to become a celebrity, when society is ridden with not just ambition but also aggression to achieve fame or power, the qualities of Narain's persona tell us well how he, as a poet, kept himself so far from these things...*'[4]

Indeed, he has been variously called 'the Buddha of contemporary poetry',[5] a purist, a secular mystic—but, above all, a true poet, who lives poetry as much as he writes it. It is this aspect of a life lived in poetry that underlies the distinctive ontology of his work.

*

Narain's oeuvre spans seven decades and diverse genres. Within poetry too, a range exists—from longer poems to aphorisms and couplets, from Sanskrit and Urdu to English and French

---

[4] Geet Chaturvedi, '*Unse Lambā Unkī Kavitā Kā Jīvan*', in *Hindustān*, 16 Nov. 2017 (translated from the Hindi)

[5] Pankaj Chaturvedi, '*Samkālīn Kavitā Ke Buddha Kā Jānā*', in *Lamhī*, Jan. 2018 (translated from the Hindi)

inspirations, from meditative and metaphysical works to those drawing on mythology and history, and from motifs of nature and the personal to the rough and tumble of the socio-political and the contemporary, with the many enigmas and overlaps in between. It is perhaps linked to what Harish Trivedi calls '*a poetic sensibility which is exceptionally diverse culturally and historically... He is a thinking poet, a widely read and travelled poet, a 'historical' poet (on the pattern of a 'historical' novelist), a literary poet (in the sense of being engaged with literary traditions), a cosmopolitan poet (as being abreast with world literature) and above all a poet of deep humanism, with a rare degree of moral discrimination as well as sympathy... He observes this world acutely while also caring for it tenderly, and the scope of his humanism is not limited to human beings but extends to birds and animals and indeed to all of creation.*' Narain read extensively, across literatures, languages and disciplines, as his library of over 20,000 books would testify, and Upanishadic, Buddhist, Sufi, Western and Marxist thought all played a role. But, '*what distinguished him is that this Western stimulus is embedded in his assiduously cultivated knowledge of the 3,500-year old tradition of Indian literature...*'[6]

His poetic style saw a major change in the sixties, as a poet of the *Nayī Kavitā* (New Poetry) that broke away from the romantic *Chāyāvād* tradition—though he was never really besotted with 'movements'. The poems here limn Narain's later poetic voice, in contrast to his more overtly complex, symbolist and imagist style of the fifties. In fact, after his very first collection, *Cakravyūh*, he began tearing down the wall of language. In later collections, poems combine more

---

[6] Harish Trivedi, 'Introduction: An Embedded Cosmopolitan', in Kunwar Narain, *No Other World: Selected Poems,* trans. Apurva Narain, Arc Publications, UK, 2010

accessible exteriors with far-reaching, nuanced content, without attempting to startle or distract with affectation of any kind. This transitional direction may well suggest an intentional process of poetic evolution more generally. In his introduction to Borges' selected poems, for instance, di Giovanni says, '*As a poet, Borges has striven over the years to write more and more clearly, plainly, and straightforwardly*', moving '*away from callow, tiresome, and merely clever inventiveness*', even preferring more common metaphors instead of new ones—for in Borges' own words, '*really good metaphors are always the same*'.[7]

Narain too at times blends visionary or mnemonic content with deceptively simple metaphors and constructs, devoid of ornateness. The poems here are often austere on the surface but slowly expansive in their evocations. In them, he visualises '*a strange book / that had no loops of language, / the biggest of ideas were tiny / little word-sized images…*'[8] The poems evolve with a reader's patience, even love, inviting her to dwell on them. As in *No Other World*, 'the experiment is often conducted not in the lurid exteriors of a poem but in its inner recesses', resonating long after. For the poet, the process is almost akin to an easy but profound conversation: '*When I sit down to write, someone else also comes and sits near me… at the distance of a dialogue. A conversation goes on with that person, who is difficult to identify. She or he could be anyone intimately known to me; a reader, critic or scholar; or just my alter ego. A reminiscence of that talk remains…*'[9] This is a window to the poet's technique, and also to a translator's task.

---

[7] Jorge Luis Borges, *Selected Poems 1923-1967*, ed. Norman Thomas di Giovanni, Penguin Modern Classics, 1985 (first published 1972)

[8] From the poem 'Some Days in Another Time, Another Place'

[9] Kunwar Narain, '*Bhāṣā Ke Dhruvāntoṁ Tak : Vājaśravā Ke Bahāne*' (To the Polar Ends of Language: On Vajashrava's Pretext), in *Śabd Aur Deśkāl*, Rajkamal, 2013 (translated from the Hindi)

*

This book of translations of Narain's poetry comes after *No Other World*. While poems in the latter were selected from five original collections published between 1956 and 2002, the poems here are selections from five books between 1979 and 2018. Most are from *Hāśiye Kā Gavāh* (*Witness in the Margin*, 2009) and the posthumous *Sab Itnā Asamāpt* (*All So Unfinished*, 2018)—both published after *No Other World* (2008)—and some from three earlier collections, *Apne Sāmne* (*In Front of Us*, 1979), *Koī Dūsrā Nahīṁ* (*No One the Other*, 1993), and *In Dinoṁ* (*These Days*, 2002). With about a hundred poems, the book is divided into eight sections—each starting with a picture of one of the poet's belongings, and a short poem or excerpt. Poems published before 1979, excerpts from his three book-length poems, and poems in *No Other World*, are not included here.

In a way, this introduction thus continues on from *No Other World*—and, where possible, access to that will give the reader a fuller picture. Facts about the poet's life and works, or aspects of the translation process in relation to his work discussed there (I had invoked Walter Benjamin then in this context) [10] are not repeated. They remain relevant here. Instead, I have largely tried to stay with the poems in this selection, their contexts and their connections.

Several poems here, born from a memory, internalise past experiences... and then, go beyond them. It was instructive for me to prod my father on some and, on occasion, I have included a note even if the original did not carry it. Often, especially for

[10] Walter Benjamin, 'The Task of the Translator: An Introduction to the Translation of Baudelaire's Tableaux Parisiens', in *Illuminations*, trans. Harry Zohn, ed. Hannah Arendt, Fontana, 1973

earlier poems, he did not recollect these well, and I have not indicated anything either. But it was interesting to learn, for instance, that the film *Easy Rider* may have triggered something for a poem like 'Post Mortem of a Phoenix', or that 'Some Days in Another Time, Another Place' may have had a bit to do with his long stay with me in Cambridge, UK. Poems recall a place, person or period; these are then universalised. In other works, such as his epical poems—two based on Upanishadic episodes related to Nachiketa and Vajashrava, and one on the Buddhist scholar-translator Kumarajiva—such personal or metaphysical introspection is conflated with mythology and history in modern moulds. By comparison, the poems here are purer 'witnesses of remembrance'.

*

The larger worldviews that seem to underpin some of Narain's approach become increasingly important as one moves through more and more of his work. As alluded to earlier, one begins to understand how some of the poems add up to more than themselves… I have discussed this at some length in the afterword to *The Play of Dolls*, in the context of his stories.[11] But it may be fruitful to briefly mention it here as well.

For Narain, the absurdity of fundamentally transactional constructs that the world has evolved into or been abstracted into (the fabricated, unmoderated 'realities' of money, business, machine, law, office, nation, identity and so many other devices of intrusion and exploitation that we first create, and then trap ourselves in), is a central concern… peace is transacted in shops, people become numbers, and truths become machines. It is a

---

[11] Kunwar Narain, *The Play of Dolls: Stories*, trans. John Vater and Apurva Narain, Penguin Modern Classics, India, 2020

sharp contrast to the possibility of a simple, *'sahaj'* world where action is not motivated by expectation, payback or territorialism. Unwilling to deal with the world on its hardened terms—he nevertheless does not give up on a visionary, unremitting hope for it. His life and work, in their collective personas, seem to be constructing a paradigm around this hope. The poet Muktibodh alluded to it way back in 1961, drawing a link to Narain's own life in literature—by also refusing to look at literature as a 'transactional field', Narain was rather unique in his stance. [12]

The protagonists of some poems here are also bewildered by the faces of the warring, competitive world they get trapped in. The moral wildernesses of civilisation are conflated with surreal, silent injustices in poems like 'Groundwork' and 'A Peaceful War'. But this does not mean disaffection for the world. *'The redemptive possibilities for him, however distant or infinite, perhaps lie in how we constitute the self, in unison with the 'other' . . . the idea of the other is demolished and merged with a larger construct of the self, personified and personalised by embracing it, existing in it and extending it to a whole universe within and outside.'* [13]

In his long poem *Kumarajiva*, he says that once a child sets foot on earth, the entire earth becomes its mother. This oneness with the larger world, inherent in the ideas of non-dualism and inter-being, is a leitmotif across some poems. By anthropomorphising a tree, bird, door, stone, wind, sky, water . . . the poet also seems to put some sort of a moral onus on us. In a story, he says: *'But she who beats her head outside in pain,*

---

[12] Gajanan Madhav Muktibodh, 'The Troubled Conscience of an Afflicted Soul', in *Indian Literature*, *305*, Sahitya Akademi, May-June 2018, trans. Alka Tyagi, from the Hindi *'Antarātmā Kī Pīṛit Vivek-Chetnā'*, an essay on Narain's *Parivéś : Ham-Tum*, 1961
[13] Apurva Narain, Afterword, in Kunwar Narain, *The Play of Dolls*

she is only the wind—she won't understand what I'm saying. Yet, I exist because of her—somewhat so, that I will have to understand what she's saying… Rising quietly, I open the shuttered doors, and embrace that primal, rugged tempest to my breast.[14] This is similar to what happens in a poem like 'Invitation' or 'Un-Distances' …it is we who must understand, we who must hear.

From a translator's viewpoint, these considerations mean that the quiddities of individual poems must not eclipse a sense of the larger worldviews being constructed, and vice versa—while also being attentive to what the poet calls the 'memories' of words, and not just their meanings. This often required a certain precision with choosing words that evoked, rather than blurred, a multiplicity of intents.

*

It was edifying for me to keep in mind that translating too, indeed like praying or loving or writing, is perhaps better directed at changing oneself than wishing for something… allowing oneself to be humbled and moulded by the unknown, by the entity or poem in front of us, than wishing a new life for it… and if a new and beautiful life is nevertheless born, it is perhaps because of the transformation wrought in us rather than by us. Indeed, these poems changed me more than I changed them.

As mentioned, there is not much overt linguistic legerdemain in the poems—they are profound without being smart or sensational. Like them, their translations had to whisper rather than shout out their presence. Translating this easy, open quality was exacting work—like in the original too, the poet's effortless style perhaps entailed much effort. As his Estonian translator

---

[14] Kunwar Narain, 'Near and Around Shapes', in *The Play of Dolls*

Margus Lattik puts it, this is an *'arrived at simplicity... with great depths... beyond complexity'.* [15] Translating it involved treading the full spectrum between manic precision and fanciful licence across different poems.

In Kunwar Narain, each reading of a poem can throw up new layers of meaning or allusion, new whispers and tints, new disquiets, new calms... his sister can become the image of melancholy, a bird can acquire godliness, nature and lover can begin to seem like one. His technique often brings together soul and universe, feminine and masculine, thought and emotion... the *'ham'* in his poems can often be me or us, the *'vah'* can be she or he, the *'man'* can be mind or heart... and not just because the Hindi allows it. Translating such instances into the English was interesting, linguistically and poetically, and I took substantial liberties on occasion... changing, for example, from first to third person, or singular to plural, where context or content prodded. Likewise, moving away from the literal translation of a title or phrase, altering the visual structure or rhyme scheme in a poem, or, conversely, adhering closely to the rhythm or syntax of the original—or not—have been, like in any translation, subjective choices.

Echoing the poet's own mind, it meant eclecticism—taking different positions in different poems (the choice dictated by the poem itself, by its 'semantic dominant'), which then averaged out to a sort of 'middle path'. Thus, faithfully mirroring a poem's *intent*—a truer correspondence to its inner embrace—became more important than fidelity or freedom per se. Choices concerning end-stopped or enjambed lines, syllable

---

[15] Margus Lattik, 'Operating Multiple Frequencies of Time', in *Indian Literature, 308*, Sahitya Akademi, India, Nov-Dec 2018

or accent counts, punctuation and capitalisation, alliteration and anaphora, were largely guided by the poem in question, and to an extent by my own predilections, but only rarely by *a priori* considerations. As in my earlier translations, such choices vary significantly across poems.

*

As is often said, the poet doesn't choose her or his poems; they choose the poet. For a poet like Narain, doggedly wedded to his conscience, this is indeed true. The poems defy categorisation. Alongside a thematic and stylistic range, his verse is varyingly intellectual, interrogative, meditative, elliptical... at times even cinematic. There is little reportage or doctrine in his poetry; his politics derives more from ethics than any camp ideology, and his rebellion is more fundamental than 'within the construct'.

Narain tries to reinstate the sublime values of the human and natural worlds to literature; of patience, moderation and giving. It is difficult to believe that a way of life that is increasingly frenetic, and simmering with the violence of ambition and speed-obsessed activity, does not erode a certain poetry of life. It leaves no time to ponder, so to say, at the interstices between lines. Narain's poetry, in this sense, is an exploration of that original calm, the pristine expanse, which one tries to re-create and restore, inside and outside. This is also an ecological imperative—greed is as much a human as an ecological sin—and a feature of his poetry is how the human and the ecological coalesce in it, how our inter-being becomes 'the wish of a leaf'.

In some of the poems, he seems to say, '*I do not imitate nature, I am nature... we live in two worlds: one that each creates,* one created by all together... "*my*" *world may or may not differ from ours*.'[16] He sardonically laments a kind of helplessness in the face of evolution itself when he says, '*I reached this world a little late*', and a quest for what it really means to be human runs through many poems. I had invoked the neologism *humanesque* for this in *No Other World*, not humanism in a rationalist sense but humanity both generous and vulnerable. It is not a tradition that privileges humans over others, or one human over another; instead it draws from a wisdom that allows us to moderate our needs and desires in acceptance of the other.

In the love poems, even those with erotic elements, wider human or ecological solicitudes are not eclipsed—they are enlarged instead, by love's potential as a ubiquitous poetic language. On his technique, he says '*When I doubt a poem's structure, I look at life. Life's real power lies in its flexibility, not rigidity... this is also a basis for my creativity. When varied life experiences are given a free span, they seem to form a pattern of their own...*'[17] This is also how he recalls fragments from past experiences of love, '*which we, somehow, piece together / to again create a new / language of love*'.[18] It entails an intimacy that bridges over from poet to reader, where poetry and remembrance themselves become languages of love. In them, he also celebrates the anonymity of life, of the ordinary and the unnoticed... for it is the anonymity of love that perhaps ultimately sustains. In a poem, he says that no one is ordinary, that 'the ordinary' is only 'the distant', and the effort not to be ordinary is, in fact, the effort to be distant towards none.[19]

---

[16] Kunwar Narain, Prologue in *Parives : Ham-Tum*
[17] Kunwar Narain, '*Bhāṣā Ke Dhruvāntoṁ Tak*', in *Śabd Aur Deśkāl*
[18] From the poem 'The Languages of Love'
[19] Kunwar Narain, '*Koī Ādamī Māmūlī Nahīṁ Hotā*', in *Koī Dūsrā Nahīṁ*

It was a language like this that journalist Ravish Kumar perhaps had in mind when he wrote: '*It is time to bid farewell to the aggression that we have allowed in our language over the past years. How I wish that the manner in which a good and soft-spoken poet speaks would prevail. These days, now and then, I start reading the poetry of Kunwar Narain. I do not know why, but I feel that this poet can lead us to the door of a new language. His language urges gentleness, and makes us practice anonymity. How I wish that our politics, our society, all of us, would establish a poet's language publicly. How much nicer this would be.*'[20]

History interests Narain. He says, '*Every piece of writing… is historical. This past can be part of a moment before or thousands of years ago; we revive it in memory and seek a new relation with it, giving it a new life, reconstructing it in language… A bridge is created between the writer and the reader, and also amongst readers.*'[21] He sees as a detached observer, in the spirit of Kabir, and sees more emancipation in our cultural and social history than in political history. He sees hope in the history of people's daily struggles, and in 'a third history' of reconciliations. For history is not divorced from the present for him; it is a window to us, now.

Time, in its variegated constructs, is a recurrent trope in his work; these poems also often transcend geographical and temporal boundaries. They transpose impressions, and a certain '*jijīvishā*' (the will to live—a concept very dear to the poet), from decades and centuries ago into today's milieu, such as

[20] Ravish Kumar, '*Kyā Is Samay Aur Samāj Ko Ek Naī Bhāṣā Kī Zarūrat Nahīṁ…?*' in *khabar.ndtv.com*, updated: 2 June 2020 (translated from the Hindi); accessed 8 January 2021, at: https://khabar.ndtv.com/news/blogs/ravish-kumar-blog-on-coronavirus-pandemic-impact-over-society-and-time-2239228
[21] Kunwar Narain, '*Bhāṣā Ke Dhruvāntoṁ Tak*', in *Śabd Aur Deśkāl*

in the ekphrastic 'Guernica' or in the poems on Hikmet and Neruda. The latter two recall formative literary experiences from over half a century ago—when, as a young man, the poet spent time with them and other writers during a long trip through post-war Europe, Russia and China. The long gestation period between the event and the poem signals the poet's own unhurried, hesitant world, as also a space-time continuum across which a certain past acquires relevance today in some universal, yet personal, reinvention of itself.

The last decade, when some of the poems in this book were written, was a time of suffering for the poet, riddled with age and blindness. Of course, sorrow spares no one, and he too knew it from a young age. But each time he endured pain or injustice, he never failed to forgive, forget, love back more... The remarkable thing for me—and a context for some poems—is how completely free he was of hate, envy, greed... of all the 'sins'; indifferent to praise or scorn, beautiful in the face of sorrow. In a lifetime with him, I never once saw him get angry, talk ill of anyone, or even swat a fly. Instead, he turned to the cosmos within, marvelling at the paradox of god in a godless world, the numen of nature in us, and the moral as an evolutionary counterpoise to the physical. Gnomic compositions like 'The Prize', 'No One Else' and 'E&OE', or some personal poems in the later sections, are auto-reflections that call to mind some of these motifs, imbued with sorrow, serenity and enigma at once.

In other poems, it is as if he were saying: '...*colour, fragrance, rasa... are all ethereal. They grow out of the earth and move towards the sky like a flower, then dissipate into the sky itself... What we touch is only their body basis... Beauty, like nature's splendour, incarnates in the physical; then, returning what is earth to earth, evanesces. We can preserve copies of its shapes, memories of its semblances, in coarse physicality, but can only realise its essence in feelings… it appears through a medium and stays saved in our imagination and memory even when the medium is not there. It leaves behind a melancholic image. The poem is as much a poem of this melancholy as it is of its elixir and gaiety.'* [22]

Here, 'remembering' and 'mourning' acquire significance not just as metaphors of translation but also, for several poems, as contextual pivots. [23] In the process, the poems leave us redeemed and restless all at once.

*

Acknowledgements

Journals first carried several of the poems here. Acknowledgements are due to the editors of *Asymptote, Modern Poetry in Translation, KIN, Asia Literary Review, Life and Legends, Dhauli Review, Scroll, Indian Literature, The Indian Quarterly, City, deLuge Journal* and *Columbia Journal*.

I wish to thank the Estonian poet and translator of Narain's poems, Mathura M. Lattik, for his suggestions on this book early on. In a way, this also helped me resume a long-pending task. I am grateful to Jean Boase-Beier, my editor for *No Other World;* her inputs here allowed some continuity across the two books. Thanks to John Vater, my co-translator on *The Play of Dolls*, for our interactions on the craft of translation there—

[22] Kunwar Narain, in an interview in *Jiye Hue Se Zyādā: Kũvar Nārāyaṇ Ke Sāth Saṁvād*, conversations with Kunwar Narain, Rajkamal Prakashan, Delhi, 2023 (translated from the Hindi)

[23] Paul Ricouer, 'Translation as Challenge and Source of Happiness', in *On Translation*, translated by Eileen Brennan, introduced by Richard Kearney, Routledge, London–New York, 2006 (French original published in 2004)

some surely rubbed off on this book too. And, of course, my heartfelt gratitude to Kanishka Gupta for taking this book first to Westland and then to Penguin; and to my editor Karthik Venkatesh, at both places, for his inputs and immense cooperation in the time of a pandemic.

This work has lingered on for a decade. Various personal fronts ruled these difficult years, and I got back to this book only recently. Brief windows did allow some work before that; I especially cherish my stays in the hills above Rishikesh, and at the Translation House Looren in Switzerland. In the last couple of years, Teena Gill's support and inputs have meant a lot to me in various ways—I am truly grateful to her.

It will remain a regret that several of the author's books could not come out in front of him, including this one. It is also a travesty of nature that, in later years, Kunwar Narain lost his eyesight, limiting his involvement in this book; yet, ironically, he at first engaged more with it than he had with *No Other World*—patiently hearing out the translations, and commenting on occasion. My mother, Bharati Narain, helped us both, my father and I, cope with all these years in untold ways, giving as only she could. My parents, like me, are a part of this book. And, like me, this book owes its existence to them.

—Apurva Narain

As If the World Were Real

As if the world were open, to achieve
...a mask, to deceive
As if the world were real, worth getting
...a waste, worth nothing

And all this was becoming and unbecoming in someone
who was laughing with one eye and weeping with one

उतना ही असमाप्त

अगर मैं सचाई हूँ
तो कुछ भी खोया नहीं।

घूमते-फिरते जिन जगहों में वास किया
वहाँ यदि लौटूँ तो
अपने को कोई नयी पहचान दे सकता हूँ
पुनः आरंभ हो सकता हूँ किसी भी संकल्प से
उतना ही सही, उतना ही प्रामाणिक,
उतना ही आदि जीवन
जो नष्ट नहीं होता,
नया होता चलता है क्रम।
        एक शक्ति
        जो न चाहती, न पछताती,
        न जिसके लिए
        केवल घटनाओं और संपर्कों की अपेक्षा
        बीतते रहने की मजबूरी।

सोचता हूँ जिस शून्य को
वह भी आकांक्षी है उसी भौतिक स्पर्श का
जिसने मुक्त किया था
अकेले स्रष्टा को उसके अकेलेपन से,
और ढाल दी थी पृथ्वी पर अकूत जीवन-राशि।

एक स्वतंत्र वर्तमान और अनिश्चित भविष्य
जो मैं हूँ
और वह सब जो अभी हो सकता हूँ

Amaranthine

If I am the truth,
nothing has been lost.

Drifting about, if I return
to the places I lived before
I can beget myself anew
begin from a resolve again:
as much right as much real
as much primal life
that does not perish,
a sequence ever-renewing…
    a will
      that neither yearns nor repents
      nor is constrained
      to only keep passing
      by people and events.

The void that I contemplate
covets that same worldly touch
which had liberated
the lonely creator of his loneliness
and had unleashed
a bounty of life on earth.

An unfettered now, an uncertain future
that I am
and all that I can still be

यदि अपने को टूटने न दूँ,
अपने को किसी तरह दूसरों से बाँधे हुए
एक अदम्य साहस—एक ढीठ उत्सव।

हमारे पास एक भाषा है
जिसमें मैंने जीना सीखा—
तुम सोचते हो इसलिए लगता है
कहीं न कहीं तुम्हारे शब्द
मेरी इच्छाओं को व्यक्त करते हैं।

हम मिलते हैं
कभी युद्धों की छाया में
कभी शान्त वनों में
खोजते हुए
मैत्री के उन सबसे मार्मिक सूत्रों को
जो सही अर्थों में वैश्विक हों।

हम खड़े हैं
एक निर्धारित समझौते की
चमकती सन्धि-रेखा पर,
जो तलवार की धार की तरह पैनी है।

कितना रहस्यमय है तुम्हारा स्पर्श
कि इतना जीकर भी उतना ही प्यासा हूँ,
इतना पाकर भी उतना ही आकांक्षी,
सब कुछ जान कर भी उतना ही अनभिज्ञ,
बार बार चाही हुई चीज़ों को
भरपूर पाकर भी उतना ही अतृप्त,
हर क्षण समाप्त होते हुए भी
उतना ही असमाप्त।

if I don't let myself break
somehow   holding on to others,
a dogged courage, a brazen carnival.

We have a language
in which I learnt to live—
you think, so it feels
your words somewhere
speak my desires.

We meet
sometimes in the shadow of wars
sometimes in tranquil forests, searching
the most sentient codes of amity
that are truly universal.

We stand
on the shimmering truce line
of a covenant,
sharp like the blade of a sabre.

How mysterious your touch

that I am
still as thirsty after living so much
still as desirous after having so much
still as unknowing after knowing all

as unfulfilled after getting
things longed for again and again,
as unending even after
each moment ending.

संदर्भ : गुएर्निका

मैं जो सोचता हूँ उसे चिन्तित करता हूँ, केवल उसे नहीं जो देखता हूँ
—पिकासो

मुश्किल होता है
एक कुचली हुई शक्ल का
चित्र में पुनर्वास ठीक वैसा ही
जैसा वह पहले था,
टूटे-फूटे को टुकड़ा-टुकड़ा जोड़ कर
फिर वैसा ही रचना जैसा वह था।

इससे बेहतर है ध्वस्त को ढहा कर
उसके मलबे से
नया कुछ बनाना...

एक आँख बची थी
उसमें कुछ रोशनी
रोशनी में कुछ जीवन-संकेत

होठों से चिपके दाँतों में
चिपकी थी अभी तक एक हँसी
बच्चे-सी

चेहरे के चिथड़ा भूगोल में
खिड़कियों की तरह खुले
दो कानों के बीच
दस फ़ीसदी मस्तिष्क की स्थिति
चिंताजनक थी

Guernica

I paint objects as I think them, not as I see them
—*Picasso*

How arduous
to restore in a painting
a mangled face
    to exactly what it was before,
to piece together
the shattered pieces
and re-create them
    as they were before.

Better to raze the ruins
and from the rubble
    create something anew...

An eye was saved
in it some light
    some signs of life in the light

In the teeth clinging to lips
still clung a laughter
    child-like

In the tattered geography of a face
between two ears open like windows
a ten percent nook for the mind's situation
    was disconcerting

नाक को खींच कर सीधा किया जा सकता था
जीभ की लंबाई तक
लेकिन ऊँचा नहीं

बाक़ी जिस्म
सिर के नीचे का वह तहस-नहस ढाँचा था
जिसे वहीं का वहीं लगाने के बजाय
कहीं का कहीं लगाया जा सकता था...

कुल मिलाकर
जो एक अन्देशे का चित्र उभरता
वह एक आदमी का भी हो सकता है
और दुनिया का भी।

A nose could be pulled and straightened
up to the length of a tongue
        but not raised

The rest of the body
was a mauled-up frame under the head—
that instead of being put right there
could be put from any to anywhere
        to salvage what remained...

All in all
the unsaid picture that emerged
from the peril of an apocalypse
        could always be
        of a being
        and also of a world.

इन्तिज़ाम

कल फिर एक हत्या हुई
अजीब परिस्थितियों में ।

मैं अस्पताल गया
लेकिन वह जगह अस्पताल नहीं थी ।
वहाँ मैं डॉक्टर से मिला
लेकिन वह आदमी डॉक्टर नहीं था ।
उसने नर्स से कुछ कहा
लेकिन वह स्त्री नर्स नहीं थी ।
फिर वे ऑपरेशन-रूम में गए
लेकिन वह जगह ऑपरेशन-रूम नहीं थी ।
वहाँ बेहोश करनेवाला डॉक्टर
पहले ही से मौजूद था—मगर वह भी
दरअसल कोई और था ।

फिर वहाँ एक अधमरा बच्चा लाया गया
जो बीमार नहीं, भूखा था ।

डॉक्टर ने मेज़ पर से
ऑपरेशन का चाकू उठाया
मगर वह चाकू नहीं
ज़ंग लगा भयानक छुरा था ।

छुरे को बच्चे के पेट में भोंकते हुए उसने कहा
अब यह बिल्कुल ठीक हो जायगा ।

Groundwork¹

Another execution yesterday
Under peculiar circumstances.

I went to a hospital
But the place was not a hospital.
I met a doctor there
But the person was not a doctor.
He whispered something to a nurse
But the nurse was not a nurse.
Then they went inside
An operating theatre but it was
Not an operating theatre.
An anaesthetist was already there
To etherise—but in fact
Even he was someone else.

Then a half-dead child was brought in
Not ailing, but starving.

At the table, the doctor
Picked up a surgical knife.
Not a surgical knife
But a rusty, ominous dagger.

Thrusting it into the child's stomach
He assured—
Now all will be well.

सोने का नगर

वह तलछट है जहाँ आत्मदया, परिप्रेक्ष्य में
ज़िन्दगी नहीं
ज़िन्दगी की रट पर चढ़ी हुई कच्ची रंगमयता
जो छूटती चली गयी

काम और नाकाम में विभाजित
अपने कुल किये का भाग्यफल
अपनी ही अंगमयता के लिए लालायित।
वही जो रोज़-रोज़ होता
पर व्यतीत नहीं होता है। एक अनुभव—
तमाम अनुभवों को चबाकर नीरस
थूक रहा हूँ जो शब्दों के खोखल। साँस भर
ताक़त छटपटाने के लिए
उस ज़मीन पर विजय पाने के लिए
जिसे जीतने धूम से निकले थे
हवा को रौंदते घुड़सवार
और स्वर्ग के स्वामी इन्द्र ने
किये थे उल्का से प्रहार...

हाँ, परिचित हूँ उस ज़मीन से
जो भीग गयी थी हवाई बादलों से,
और देख रहा हूँ बुझी आँखों से
उस धधकते आकाश को भी
जहाँ शताब्दियाँ झुलस जाती हैं।

City of Gold

This settling sediment of self-pity,
in perspective, is not life
but short-lived colour
coated on the rut of life
that kept flaking off

Sundered into the useful and useless,
the zodiac result of one's doing
slavering over one's own bonhomie.
That which happens daily
but does not pass. An experience—
many experiences chewed dry, spat out
like hollowed hulls of words. A breathful
of fizz to flounder around,
to win that ground
for which horsemen had set out
with so much fanfare
marauding the air,
and the lord of heaven Indra
had also struck with meteors...

Yes, I know that ground
which airy clouds had drenched,
and I am watching with blurry eyes
that blazing sky
where centuries get scorched.

पहली दिग्विजय का वह भूरा धुँधला फाटक
धोखा था—पहला धोखा—जिसके बाद
सोने का नगर नहीं
केवल एक उजाड़ रूखी वापसी।

That grey foggy gate of first victory
was a deception—the first deception—after which
there was no city of gold,
only a desolate return, dour as dust.

पत्थर के प्राण

पहली चोट पड़ते ही
पत्थर से ध्वनित हुआ   आह

इससे जाना कि पत्थरों में भी
होते हैं प्राण।

कहाँ बसते हैं ये प्राण
यह जानने के लिए

चोटें पहुँचाता रहा
सधे हुए हाथों से मूर्तिकार।

पूरी मूर्ति को एक शिला से
काट कर बाहर निकाल लिया

तब जाना शिला के हृदय को
जहाँ एक घाव बचा रह गया था।

मूर्तिकार देख रहा था अपने
लहूलुहान हाथों को...

The Beings of Stones

I saw the angel in the marble, and carved until I set him free
— *Michelangelo*

at the very first blow
the stone resounded   *aah*

from this one learnt
stones also have lives

to know where
their pneumas reside

the sculptor kept striking
with dexterous hands

he created a whole statue
cutting it out of a rock

and only then could
come to know

a rock's heart
was where a wound remained…

the sculptor was looking at his
blood-sodden hands

गले तक धरती में

गले तक धरती में गड़े हुए भी
सोच रहा हूँ
कि बँधे हों हाथ और पाँव
तो आकाश हो जाती है उड़ने की ताक़त

जितना बचा हूँ
उससे भी बचाए रख सकता हूँ यह अभिमान
कि अगर नाक हूँ
तो वहाँ तक हूँ जहाँ तक हवा
मिट्टी की महक को
हलकोर कर बाँधती
फूलों की सूक्तियों में
और फिर खोल देती
सुगन्धि के न जाने कितने अर्थों को
हज़ारों मुक्तियों में

कि अगर कान हूँ
तो एक धारावाहिक कथानक की
सूक्ष्मतम प्रतिध्वनियों में
सुन सकने का वह पूरा सन्दर्भ हूँ
जिसमें अनेक प्रार्थनाएँ और संगीत
चीखें और हाहाकार
आश्रित हैं एक केन्द्रीय ग्राह्यता पर

Buried in the Earth Up to the Neck

buried in the earth up to the neck,
she thinks
with arms and legs trussed up
her strength to fly
becomes a sky

from whatever remains of her
she could keep an esteem saved—

that if she were a nose
she'd be up to where the breeze
stirs up and tethers a whiff of earth
to the hymns of flowers
and then opens up
manifold meanings of fragrance
to a thousand freedoms

if she were the ears
then in the faintest muffled echoes
of an unceasing tale
she'd be that whole milieu of listening
in which untold prayers and songs,
cries and wails, seek to be heard
untrammelled

अगर ज़बान हूँ
तो दे सकता हूँ ज़बान
ज़बान के लिए तरसती ख़ामोशियों को—
शब्द रख सकता हूँ वहाँ
जहाँ केवल निःशब्द बेचैनी है

अगर ओठ हूँ
तो रख सकता हूँ मुझी\ति ओठों पर भी
क्रूरताओं को लज्जित करती
एक बच्चे की विश्वासी हँसी का बयान

अगर आँखें हूँ
तो तिल-भर जगह में भी
वह सम्पूर्ण विस्तार हूँ
जिसमें जगमगा सकती हैं असंख्य सृष्टियाँ...

गले तक धरती में गड़े हुए भी
जितनी देर बचा रह पाता है सिर
उतने समय को ही अगर
दे सकूँ एक वैकल्पिक शरीर
तो दुनिया से करोड़ों गुना बड़ा हो सकता है
एक आदमक़द विचार।

if she were a tongue
she could give her word—
her voice to the silences
that yearn for a voice—
put words where there's only
a wordless disquiet

if she were the lips
she could put upon wilting lips
the testimony of a child's trustful smile
that puts all spite to shame

if she were the eyes
then even in a speckle of the iris
she'd be that entirety of expanse
where countless creations can glimmer...

even buried in the earth up to the neck,
if she could give another body
to just as much time
as the head upholds itself

then a billion times bigger
than the world could be
a humanesque idea

आधे मिनट का एक सपना

पुराने ज़मानों की नहीं
इसी सदी की कोई किताब थी,
   पढ़ते-पढ़ते कब झपकी आ गई
   पता ही न चला...
   मेरी पत्नी वहीं कहीं आसपास थी :

मैं फ़ौजी पोशाक में था
पोशाक पर कलफ़ इतना कड़क था
कि उसमें अगर मैं न भी होता
तो भी वह उसी तरह
अकड़ कर खड़ी रहती
   और जब मैं चलता तो वह
   फ़ौजी बूटों की तरह चरमराती :

मैंने पत्नी की तरफ़ देखा
और बाक़ायदा एक सैल्यूट किया।
   पत्नी ने कहा—बकवास,
   और अख़बार पढ़ती रही।

फ़ौजी ताक़त की यह उपेक्षा
   दंडनीय थी :
   एक धमाका हुआ
   और घर की छत
   दीवारों सहित उड़ गई!

अब वहाँ केवल मैं था
   और वह थी।

The Half a Minute Dream

It was some book
not of bygone times but of this century,
    I do not even know
        when I dozed off reading it...
my wife was nearby:

I was in a soldierly uniform
so stiff and so crackingly starched
that even if I were not in it
it would still keep standing swaggeringly erect
in exactly the same way,
    and when I walked it would
        creak like martial boots.

I looked at my wife
and saluted as per protocol.
    She said—nonsense,
    and kept reading the news.

This undermining of regimental authority
meant retribution—
    there was a big bang
    and the roof of the house blew away
    together with the walls.

Now, only I was there
    and she was there.

कुछ लोग भागते हुए आए
और हमारे सिरों के ऊपर से निकल गए
कुछ लोग उनका पीछा करते हुए आए
और हमें घेर कर खड़े हो गए;
    वे जो भी कर रहे थे
      शायद उनकी भी समझ से बाहर था,
      इस बीच बेकारी की बात उठाना
      एक संगीन जुर्म मालूम होता था!

किसी ने मेरी ओर
एक रोटी फेंकी
    उसे शक हुआ कि मुझे
    इस पर आपत्ति है।
    यह विद्रोह था...

इसी समय दूर कहीं
    बिगुल बजा,
एक बुरा सपना
आधे मिनट के टी.वी. विज्ञापन की तरह
अचानक समाप्त हो गया।

मैं फ़ौजी वर्दी से
बाहर आ गया था।
    अरगनी पर सूखते कपड़े हवा में
    सफ़ेद झंडों की तरह लहरा रहे थे
    पत्नी खाने पर बुला रही थी।

बाहर किसी गली में
शोर करते बच्चे
    पतंग उड़ा रहे थे।

Some people came scampering in
and went past above our heads,
some came hounding them and stood
all around us. In this babel
perhaps they also didn't fathom
whatever they kept doing:
  to talk of joblessness here
  seemed like a solemn offence.

Someone flung towards me
a piece of bread,
  he suspected that I
  objected to it—
  this was an all-out rebellion...

At this moment, somewhere far afield,
  a bugle sounded:

A fiendish dream
like a half-minute TV ad
ended abruptly.

I had now come out
of my military fatigues.

  Clothes drying on a washing line
  were swaying like white flags in the wind,
  my wife and I were going to have lunch.

Children making noise
outside in some lane
  were flying kites.

क्या हम सब कुछ जानते हैं

क्या हम सब कुछ जानते हैं
एक दूसरे के बारे में

क्या कुछ भी छिपा नहीं होता हमारे बीच
कुछ घृणित या मूल्यवान
जिन्हें शब्द व्यक्त नहीं कर पाते

जो एक अकथ वेदना में जीता और मरता है
जो शब्दित होता बहुत बाद
जब हम नहीं होते
एक दूसरे के सामने
और एक की अनुपस्थिति विकल हो उठती है
        दूसरे के लिए।

जिसे जिया उसे सोचता हूँ
जिसे सोचता उसे दोहराता हूँ
इस तरह अस्तित्व में आता है पुनः
जो विस्मृति में चला गया था,
जिसकी अवधि अधिक से अधिक
        सौ साल है।

एक शिला-खण्ड पर
दो तिथियाँ
बीच की यशगाथाएँ
हमारी सामूहिक स्मृतियों में
        संचित हैं।

Do We Know All [2]

Do we understand the entirety
of each other

Is there nothing that remains veiled
between us, hideous or precious,
which words fail to convey

which lives and dies in untold pain
which is uttered long after,
when we are not there
before each other
and the absence of one becomes
a purgatory for the other...

We contemplate what we lived,
relive what we contemplate, and so
what had passed into oblivion
again comes to life this way,
whose span at most
is a hundred years.

Two dates on
an epitaph,
tales of glory in between
amassed
in our collective remembrance.

कभी-कभी मिल जाती हैं
इस संचय में
व्यक्ति की आकांक्षाएँ
        और विवशताएँ

तब जी उठता है
दो तिथियों के बीच का वृत्तान्त।

In this assemblage, at times
a person's buried
dreams and desires,
fetters, despairs,
can also be chanced upon:

The saga between two dates is then
resurrected back to life.

अपने बजाय

रफ़्तार से जीते
दृश्यों की लीलाप्रद दूरी को लाँघते हुए : या
एक ही कमरे में उड़ते-टूटते लथपथ
दीवारों के बीच
अपने को रोककर सोचता जब

तेज़ से तेज़तर के बीच समय में
किसी दुनियादार आदमी की दुनिया से
हटाकर ध्यान
किसी ध्यान देनेवाली बात को,
तब ज़रूरी लगता है ज़िन्दा रखना
उस नैतिक अकेलेपन को
जिसमें बन्द होकर
प्रार्थना की जाती है
या अपने से सच कहा जाता है
अपने से भागते रहने के बजाय।

मैं जानता हूँ किसी को कानोंकान ख़बर
न होगी
यदि टूट जाने दूँ उस नाज़ुक रिश्ते को
जिसने मुझे मेरी ही गवाही से बाँध रखा है,
और किसी बातूनी मौक़े का फ़ायदा उठाकर
उस बहस में लग जाऊँ
जिसमें व्यक्ति अपनी सारी ज़िम्मेदारियों से छूटकर
अपना वकील बन जाता है।

Instead of Oneself

For Raghuvir Sahay [3]

Living fast and cutting across
skittish spans of variegated vistas, or
clumsily fluttering about
in the four-walled cage of a room,
    when I pause myself   and ponder

      between dizzying speeds, forgetting
      for a while the ways of the world,
      then it seems one has to keep alive
      that solitude of virtue, enclosed
      in which one prays
      or tells oneself the truth
      audaciously, instead
      of always running   away from oneself

Though I know
others will never know, not by a long shot,
if I let the numinous ligature snap
that binds me to my own testimony
and on some loquacious occasion, join the debate
where one absolves oneself of all duty
to become one's own advocate
      and plead—not guilty

एक 'शान्त' युद्ध

सिर्फ़ पटाख़ों और आतिशबाज़ियों से
लड़ा गया वह युद्ध। कोई हताहत नहीं,
रक्तपात नहीं, चीख़ पुकार नहीं—
जैसे बच्चों का वीडियो-खेल
बग़लवाले कमरे में कहीं।

अँधेरी रात
टूटते सितारों से लक़दक़ :
युद्ध युद्ध नहीं
बिलकुल 'शान्ति' हो जैसे,
आकाश में यों छूटते रहे बम और रॉकेट
हर्षोल्लास के फूल बरसते हों जैसे।

एक करुण प्रसंग भी था—
एक बेचारी चिड़िया
(शान्ति-कपोत नहीं!)
तेल में डूबी,
लेकिन सुखान्त नाटकों के अनुरूप
बच गई अन्ततः वह भी!

कुछ झुलसे हुए शहर
खण्डहरों से भी बदतर हालत में
यहाँ वहाँ दिखे,
मानो आदमी द्वारा नहीं
प्राकृतिक कारणों से नष्ट हुए हों—
वैसे इतिहास उनके बारे में
चाहे जो लिखे।

A Peaceful War

Cherry bombs, fire flowers, firecrackers—a war
fought with just pyrotechnics. No casualties,
no bloodshed, no scream nor wail—
like children playing a video game
somewhere in the room next door.

The black night aglitter
with splintering stars:
as though in war
there was no war,
only deep-dyed peace, a fusillade
of rockets and bombs flew the sky
showering flowers of joy.

There was a heartrending episode too—
a hapless bird (not a dove)
engulfed in runnels of oil
also got saved in the end,
like dramas with happy endings.

Some charred cities
more ashen-faced than ruins were
seen here and there, as if
not ravaged by man but by nature's course—
no matter what history
may write about them.

विजेता
हिंसा के सारे पापों, आरोपों से मुक्त
एक पवित्र धर्मयोद्धा के
प्रभामण्डल से युक्त,
तेज़ रोशनी में दमकता उसका चेहरा
जैसे सोने का एक तमग़ा
जो ख़ासतौर पर
इस विजय-परेड के लिए ही
चमकाया हुआ लगा।

बस इतना ही था समाचार—
आँखों देखे झूठ सच की पूरी कहानी :
खाड़ी-युद्ध की
हू-ब-हू विस्तृत रपट
विश्वस्त सूत्रों की ज़बानी !

The victor free
from all sins of gore, all blame,
bedecked with the gloriole
of a holy crusader,
his face effulgent in the strident light
like a medal of gold
seemingly burnished
especially for this
special victory parade.

This was all the news, that's it—
the complete tale of false 'n' true
seen on a screen: the verbatim
blow-by-blow account
of a war in the gulf
reported by trusted sources.

उत्तरदायित्व

जो भी रचा है मैंने
उसी का हिस्सा हूँ :
पूरी तरह मौजूद हैं उसमें
मेरे अन्तर्विरोध और मेरा अंतःकरण :
हर तरह उत्तरदायी हूँ
अपनी रची दुनिया के लिए :
अवगत हूँ उन तमाम कमियों और अतियों की
निरंतर आवाजाही से
जिनके लिए छूट गयी हैं गुंजाइशें
मेरे अज्ञान या मेरी लापरवाही से।

मैं ईश्वर होता तो
मुक्त कर लेता अपने को
यह कहकर कि सिद्धांततः
मैं अपनी रचनाओं से परे हूँ।

लेकिन मैं मनुष्य हूँ,
भाग नहीं सकता एक मनुष्य होने की ज़िम्मेदारियों से

निस्संकोच कहता हूँ
कि मेरा अध्यात्म प्रामाणिक नहीं,
मेरी कारीगरी में त्रुटियाँ हैं,
कलाओं में कामसूत्र के प्रक्षेप हैं,
मेरे आत्मबोध में स्थूल के हस्तक्षेप हैं,
मेरा सौन्दर्यबोध
सुडौल गढ़े पत्थरों के

I Am Answerable[4]

I am a part
of whatever I create,
my contradictions and my compunctions
are present there, and everywhere:
answerable in every way
to the world that I beget, I am
aware of the incessant traffic
of shortcomings and excesses
for which space was left
out of my carelessness
or benightedness...

If I were God
I would detach myself
saying that I am beyond
my creations

But I am human   and cannot
escape   my hominine duties

I do not hesitate to say that
my faith is not pristine,
there are flaws in my craft,
the sensual intrudes into my art,
the physical interferes with my soul,
my aesthetics is not about
well-chiselled stones that shape

चौरस आँगन—दृढ़ प्राचीरें—और गगनचुम्बी शिखर नहीं
मेरे आवेगों का वह गहन जंगल है
जिसमें जगह-जगह दैवी फिसलनों के
रोमांचक स्थल हैं।
भाषा में व्याकरण के ढीठ उल्लंघन हैं,
चिंतन में कल्पना की आवारा सैरों की भटकनें हैं...

स्वीकार करता हूँ
कि मेरी ही तरह
मेरी दुनिया भी
मानवीय है।

square courtyards, steadfast ramparts and sky-kissing spires,
it is that arcane jungle of my impulses
in which there are breathtaking interludes
of gods failing   here and there

My language has bold violations of grammar,
my thought has vagrant wanderings of imagination...

I fully accept that
just like me
this world of mine
is also human.

अन्तर्दृष्टि

कुँवर नारायण द्वारा बोलकर लिखवायी गयी आख़िरी कविता

देखने और सुनने की शक्ति
कम हो जाने के बाद से
टटोलता रहता हूँ अँधेरे में
अन्तर्दृष्टि की विरल शक्ति को खोजते हुए

ध्यान लगाने के लिए आँखें बन्द नहीं करता
मेरी प्रार्थनाएँ ही देवाशीष बन जाती हैं
अज्ञात संकेत प्रेरित करते हैं
मेरे क़दमों को एक ज्ञात भवितव्य की ओर

होठ हिलते हैं
धन्यवाद कहने के लिए
पर शब्द नहीं निकलते
वे केवल काँप कर रह जाते हैं

Inner Sight

The last poem that the poet dictated

Ever since the waning
Power of my hearing and sight
I fumble around in the dark
Looking for the strange power of insight

I don't close my eyes to meditate
My prayers themselves become benedictions
Unknown signals motivate
My steps towards a known fate

My lips move
To say thank you
But words don't come out
They just tremble and stay

Living Ordinary
Lives

Not just on the simmering equator
but also on the shivering poles of language
poetry is possible anywhere

Like on the one end touching sky heights
on the other seeking their depths
shimmering icebergs

आदमी अध्यवसायी था

'आदमी अध्यवसायी था' अगर
इतने ही की जयन्ती मनाकर
सी दी गयी उसकी दृष्टि
उसके ही स्वप्न की जड़ों से। न उगने पायी
उसकी कोशिशें। बेलोच पत्थरों के मुक़ाबले
        कटकर रह गये उसके हाथ

तो कौन संस्कार देगा
उन सारे औज़ारों को
जो पत्थरों से ज़्यादा उसको तराशते रहे।
चोटें जिनकी पाशविक खरोंच और घावों को
अपने ऊपर झेलता
और वापस करता विनम्र कर
ताकि एक रूखी कठोरता की
भीतरी सुन्दरता किसी तरह बाहर आये।

उसको छूती आँखों का अधैर्य कि वह पारस क्यों नहीं
जो छूते ही चीज़ों को सोना कर दे? क्यों खोजना पड़ता है
        मिथकों में, वक्रोक्तियों में, श्लेषों में, रूपकों में
        झूठ के उल्टी तरफ़ क्यों इतना रास्ता चलना पड़ता है
        एक साधारण सचाई तक भी पहुँच पाने के लिए?

The Hard-Working Man

'The man was hard-working'—if
only this was commemorated like a jubilee
and his vision sutured to the roots
of his own dream. No chance given
for his effort to evolve. Battling against unyielding stones
his hands were left severed…

Who then would sanctify those
innumerable tools that kept chiselling
him more than the stones?
Blows whose brute scars and wounds
he kept bearing upon his breast
to return them softened, so
the inward beauty of a cold harshness
could emerge somehow.

The impatience of eyes brushing against him—why
didn't he have the Midas touch
to transmute things into gold?
Why must one search so much
in myths, metaphors, puns, insinuations
why must one trudge such a long long road against untruth
to reach a simple truth?

शान्ति की दुकान

मुहल्ले में वह शान्ति बेचता है।
लाउडस्पीकरों की
एक दुकान है उसकी
मेरे घर से बिल्कुल लगी हुई।

सुबह सुबह मुँहअँधेरे दो घण्टे
लाउडस्पीकर न बजाने के
वह मुझसे सौ रूपये महीने लेता है।

वह जानता है कि मैं
उन अभागों में से हूँ
जो शान्ति के बिना जीवित नहीं रह सकते!

वह जानता है कि आनेवाले वक़्तों में
साफ़ पानी और साफ़ हवा से भी ज़्यादा
शान्ति की क़िल्लत रहेगी।

वह जानता है
कि क्रान्ति के ज़माने अब लद चुके :
अब उसे अपना पेट पालने के लिए
शान्ति का धन्धा अपनाना है।

मैं उसका आभारी हूँ।
भारत जैसे देश में
जहाँ क़ीमतें आसमान छू रहीं
सौ रूपये महीने की दर से
अगर दो घण्टा रोज़ भी शान्ति मिल सके
तो महँगी नहीं!

A Shop that Sells Peace⁵

He sells peace in the neighbourhood.
His shop of loudspeakers is right
next to my house.

He charges me a fee
of a hundred rupees per month
to not play the loudspeaker for two hours
at the crack of dawn.

He knows I am
among the unfortunate who
cannot live without peace.

He knows that in the times to come
peace will be a scarce commodity, rarer
than clean air or clean water.

He knows that
the age of blusterous revolutions is over:
to feed himself now, he has to be
in the business of peace.

I am beholden to him—

in a developing economy like India
where prices are sky-rocketing
if a hundred rupees per month can buy
even two hours of peace a day
it is not expensive.

पूरे की तलाश में

तुम जो कभी अपने बायें हाथ की तरह बेवकूफ़ हो
और कभी अपने दाहिने हाथ की तरह चालाक।
क्यों एक-दूसरे को एक-दूसरे के खिलाफ़
हाथों या हथियारों की तरह उठाकर
फिर वहीं के वहीं जा पहुँचते हो
   जहाँ तुम पहले ही से थे?

एक से दूसरी करवट बदलते हुए
  —मेरे सोये हाथ
मैंने अक्सर अपने पीछे सुनी है
किसी दरवाज़े के बन्द होने की आवाज़। और फिर
बहुत-सी आवाज़ों के एक साथ बन्द हो जाने की
   ख़ामोशी
ख़ामोशी जिसकी अपनी ज़बान होती है
  और भयानकता
जैसे एक मटमैली जिल्दोंवाली किताब
अचानक एक रात कहीं से खुल जाय
और बीच में दबी मिले एक कटी हुई जीभ
और वह निकल पड़े
अपने बाक़ी हिस्सों की तलाश में।

Searching for All of It

You who are at times stupid like your left hand
and at other times cunning like your right.
Why do you incite each against the other,
raising fists or taking up arms,
to then arrive at that same place
    where you already were?

Turning about from one side to the other
    —hands asleep,
I have often heard behind my back
the thunderclap of some door slamming shut. And then
    the silence
of a thousand voices shutting down together,

Silence that has a locution of its own
    and its spectral terror.
Like a book bound in dusty beige covers
that suddenly opens up from somewhere one night
and pressed inside is found
    a severed tongue
…that then comes out
and sets off in search of its remaining parts.

लोगों की क़तार में

ये तीर, तरकस, तलवार
ये जयघोष, ये गुणगान
इनकी आकांक्षाओं से परे
सुखद है यह नंगे सिर नंगे पाँव यात्रा

स्वीकार करता हूँ कि मैं सूरमा नहीं
साधारण हूँ।
क्या करूँगा शरीर पर घाव
और टूटे फूटे हथियार बटोर कर?

सविनय खड़ा हूँ सबके साथ
घातों प्रतिघातों से ऊबे हुए
लोगों की क़तार में।

वे जो आये थे
युद्ध से पहले ही
अपने ख़ेमे, तमग़े और शर्तनामा लेकर
निराश लौट गये
लड़ाकों और लड़ाइयों के प्रति
मेरे मन में कोई उत्साह न पाकर।

दुश्मनी को प्यार से निरस्त कर देनेवाले
अ-युद्ध प्रस्तावों पर
देखकर मेरे हस्ताक्षर
उन्हें सन्देह हुआ
मेरी निष्पक्षता पर।

In the Queue of People

These arrows, quivers and scimitars,
these clarions, these eulogies,
beyond their ambitions
blessed is the serene journey
of the bare-headed and bare-footed.

I accept that I'm no paladin,
that I'm ordinary;
what will I do amassing
a wreckage of weapons
and wounds on my body?

Humbly, I stand with all
in the queue of people tired
of manoeuvres and counter-manoeuvres.

They who had arrived
with their camps, covenants and regalia
even before the battle
returned crestfallen, seeing
no verve in me for war or warrior;

Seeing my signature
on pacific overtures of amity, meant
to quash animosity with love,
they became wary
of my stance to remain free.

रैली

सूरज निकला
    गाँव की तलैया में मुँह धोया
    और सब के साथ हो लिया

धूप खाती हवा में
बसों से उतरती भीड़
रामलीला के मैदान में

आसमान से उतारा एक रथ
रथ से उतारा एक महारथी
कवच कुंडल मुकुट पहने
जनता से कुछ कहने
और बाणों की तरह करता हुआ
भाषण की वर्षा
सबके सिरों के ऊपर से निकल गया !

नारे लगाता एक हुजूम   क़तार से खड़ी व्यवस्था ने
उठा और बैठ गया   राहत की साँस ली।

बारह इंच दिन जब इंच भर रह गया
राजधानी से गाँव लौटती बकवास में
    धूल फाँकता सूरज
      लाल आँखें
      थका माँदा
डूब गया फिर उसी गाँव की तलैया में
    जैसे वह दिन हुआ ही नहीं।

Rally

The sun arose,
     washed his face in the village pond
     and blended in with the others.

From the buses descended crowds
in the sunbathing air
on to the Ramlila grounds.

From the sky a chariot shimmied down,
from the chariot a gallant knight
with armour, halo and crown
to speak to the crowd,
and raining speeches like a blizzard of arrows
went away from above their ditsy heads.

A horde trumpeting slogans
got up and sat down,
the arrangements standing in queue
took a breath of relief.

When the twelve-inch day remained but an inch
amidst the bleary chatter
returning from capital to village
the dust-laden sun
     red-eyed
     dead beat
drowned again in the same village pond
     as if the day never happened at all.

मामूली ज़िंदगी जीते हुए

जानता हूँ कि मैं
दुनिया को बदल नहीं सकता,
          न लड़ कर
          उससे जीत ही सकता हूँ

हाँ लड़ते-लड़ते शहीद हो सकता हूँ
और उससे आगे
एक शहीद का मक़बरा
या एक अदाकार की तरह मशहूर...

लेकिन शहीद होना
एक बिल्कुल फ़र्क़ तरह का मामला है

बिल्कुल मामूली ज़िंदगी जीते हुए भी
लोग चुपचाप शहीद होते देखे गये हैं

Living an Ordinary Life

I know that
I can't change the world
    nor even fight it
    and win

Yes, fighting, I could become a martyr
and beyond that maybe
win a martyr's monument
or get stardom like a star...

But to be a martyr
is a totally different sort of thing

Living ordinary lives too
people have been seen
quietly getting martyred

एक दुराग्रह की हद तक

आदमी को पूरी तरह समझने के लिए
आवश्यक है
दूर-दूर तक उसके अतीत में जाना
  —एक दुराग्रह की हद तक...

केवल एक पशु-गंध को पकड़े
नाक की सीध में
अमीबा तक ही नहीं,
  पढ़ना होगा
  जीवाश्मों में संकेतित चिह्नित
  उसकी प्रकृति के पूरे पंचांग को

भटकते रहना होगा
अनिर्दिष्ट काल तक
उस विरल 'ध्वनि' के लिए
जिससे उत्पन्न हुआ था पहला 'शब्द'...

  एक वंश-वृक्ष पर
  सेब, साँप और बंदर,
  वृक्ष के नीचे
  प्रथम पुरुष और स्त्री
  —इतना संयोग काफ़ी नहीं

अखंड नक्षत्र-लोक को हलकोर कर
उन विशृंखल कड़ियों को जोड़ना होगा
जिनके सुयोग से संभव हो पाती है एक सृष्टि
  तमाम विसंगतियों के बावजूद

56

Up to the Limit of Obstinacy

To understand a person fully
it is necessary
to go a long long way, into her past
    —up to the limit of obstinacy…

    Not just trailing an animal smell
    in line with the nose
    down to the amoeba,
One will also have to read
the entire ephemeris of her existence
embedded in fossils

Will have to keep meandering
till indefinite time
seeking that singular sound
from which the first word was born

    On a genealogical tree
    an apple, a snake and a monkey,
    underneath the tree
    the first man and woman
    —this much coincidence isn't enough:

Jolting the undivided constellation of stars
one will have to join those links in disarray
whose happy conjunction
despite untold dissonances
    makes a creation possible

ख़ाली फ्रेम

एक कथ्य है उसका ख़ालीपन

जीवन अथवा मृत्यु की
किसी भी तस्वीर, किसी भी दृश्य को
        आमन्त्रित करता

उसकी अपनी असारता है और अपना सौन्दर्य
उसका अपना वीरान है और अपना ऐश्वर्य
अपनी प्रकृति—अपना यथार्थ—
अपना अवकाश और अपना असीम

वह एक शिल्प है जो शून्य नहीं
        जिसमें सब कुछ है
        एक न-होने मात्र की
        उत्कंठा में संचित

बरसों इसी तरह रहा है वह
        अनेक चित्रों के आवागमन का मंच

वह ज़मीन आज भी उर्वर है

उसके अमूर्तन में मौजूद हैं
उसकी ठंडी सतह से ढकी
        बेचैन गहराइयाँ।

Empty Frame

its emptiness speaks, inviting
any picture, any view
    of life or death

it has its vacuity and beauty
desolation and glory
its own nature, its own reality
its leisure and infinity

a creation, not a cipher,
    it has all in it
    corralled, and longing
    only not to be

like this for years, a stage
    for many a picture to transit

that ground is fertile
    even today

in its disembodiment exist
sleepless depths
wrapped up in its frigid mantle

Seven Short Poems

The Prize [6]

Written a day before the Jnanpith prize was conferred on the poet

exile and coronation
are daily pastimes of make-believe

donning a crown, the joy
that all see on my face
is only a child's mask

inside me, in fact,
somewhere far on the Saryu riverside
is the sadness of the sun
immersing itself in the waters

Staging of the Drama 'Tughlaq'
by Alkazi in Purana Qila [7]

a few old stairs
a coffin-sized throne
on a scaffolded bandstand
tumbling columns,
a gate hinged to a tottering arch
for entry and exit—

that's all,
this much of a stage was enough
to prop and play in a few hours
the complete drama of a king's life

आदमी का चेहरा

'कुली !' पुकारते ही
कोई मेरे अन्दर चौंका। एक आदमी
आकर खड़ा हो गया मेरे पास।

सामान सिर पर लादे
मेरे स्वाभिमान से दस क़दम आगे
बढ़ने लगा वह, जो कितनी ही यात्राओं में
ढो चुका था मेरा सामान।

मैंने उसके चेहरे से उसे
कभी नहीं पहचाना, केवल उस नम्बर से जाना
जो उसकी लाल कमीज़ पर टँका होता।

आज जब अपना सामान ख़ुद उठाया
एक आदमी का चेहरा याद आया।

भूल चूक लेनी देनी

कहीं कुछ भूल हो
कहीं कुछ चूक हो कुल लेनी देनी में
तो कभी भी इस तरफ़ आते जाते
अपना हिसाब कर लेना साफ़
ग़लती को कर देना मुआफ़
विश्वास बनाये रखना
कभी बन्द नहीं होंगे दुनिया में
ईमान के खाते।

A Face

'Coolie,' I called out, and someone
Was startled in me, a person
    Came and stood by me

With bags on head, ten steps ahead
Of my dignity, he started walking—
    He who had borne my burden
    On countless journeys

    I never recognised Him
    From his face, only a numbered tag
    Sewn on a flaming crimson shirt

Today, as I heaved and hefted my baggage on my own
    I remembered a face again

Errors & Omissions Excepted

If somewhere there be some mistake
or ever an error in this give and take,
any time you pass by this way
do set your tally right
forgive the oversight
keep trust:

The books of good faith will
never close in the world

आहट का उजाला

बिलकुल अँधेरा था
कि अचानक
उसके आने की आहट का उजाला
सुनाई दिया

जैसे सन्नाटे में
दूर से आती
किसी संगीत की ध्वनि

अँधेरे में
किसी ने
माचिस की एक तीली जलाई...

सीढ़ियाँ

पाँवों की पूरी ताक़त से
ज़मीन को दबाए,
हाथों की पूरी ताक़त से
हवा को पकड़े,
विजय-पताका की तरह फहराता
जब कोई बहुत तेज़ी से सीढ़ियाँ चढ़ता

मैं देखता सीढ़ियों को
चुपचाप उसके पाँवों के ख़िलाफ़
        एक एक कर नीचे उतरते

The Glow of Approaching Footsteps

it was pitch-dark
when suddenly
the glow of her footsteps approaching
    was heard there

like in the dead of silence
the echo of some dulcet music coming
    from far somewhere

in the darkness
    someone
      lit up a matchstick…

Stairways

Crushing the earth
with the full might of feet,
Clutching the air
with the firm grip of hands,
When someone steps up the stairs
very fast, hoisted
    like a flag of victory

I behold the flight of stairs,
stepping down one by one
    against his feet, silently

दरवाज़ा

दरवाज़े को छूते ही लगा
सबकी तरह उसकी भी एक दुनिया है
    एक अलग एकान्त एक अलग जीवन

वह केवल एक दीवार का हिस्सा नहीं
    अपने बाहर का दृश्य
    और अन्दर का अंतरंग भी है।

    उसके अतीत में भी हैं
    एक वृक्ष के बीज
    और एक महावन की गौरवगाथा,

जो आज एक नौकरी में विवश था

    इतनी निर्ममता से कटछँट कर भी
    सुन्दर लग रहे थे उसके शरीर पर
    उसके स्वाभिमान के रेशे!

० ० ०

The Door

Touching the door, it felt
    It also had a world like all
    A distinct solitude, a distinct life

It wasn't just a part of some wall
    But also the vista outside
    The heart inside

Its past too, had the seeds of a tree
    The legend of a grand forest

One tied up in servitude today

    Even after being so
    Heartlessly hewed and whittled down,

    On its body stood beautiful
    The woodgrain of its pride

o o o

अ-दूरियाँ

मैं तुमसे कुछ कह रहा था
जिसे वह भी सुन रहा था

खिड़की से बिलकुल सटकर बैठा था
उसका अपना एकांत
उसका अपलक आकाश
        कान लगाए
        दृष्टि गड़ाए हम पर ।

सिर्फ़ एक
        पर्दा है
            अंतर्मुखी और बहिर्मुखी के बीच

हम भी जब चाहें सुन सकते हैं
        उसकी भी बातें
            वह क्या कह रहा है
            हम से
            तुम से

Un-Distances

I say something to you
that he was hearing too

Sitting so close, right next to the window,
his tight-lipped solitude
his unblinking sky
     ear to the ground
     eyes riveted on us...

There is only   a curtain
         between
            looking inwards and outwards

We can also hear him speak
     whenever we wish to—
         what he says
         to us
           to you

ऐ हवा

ऐ हवा, ले चल मुझे
कहीं भी। साँस हूँ मैं भी
तेरी ही तरह...
पूरब पश्चिम उत्तर दक्षिण
कहीं भी

आँधी की तरह एक रात उठ
तोड़ कर मुझे वृक्ष के वक्ष से
ले चल
सागर मरुथल पर्वत घाटी
कहीं भी। एक बार
जहाँ अनुभव कर सकूँ
कि मैं केवल एक देह में क़ैद नहीं
वह प्राण हूँ
जो धड़क रहा है पूरे संसार में

Here, Wind

here, wind, ferry me away
anywhere. I am but a breath
just like you...

north and south, east or west
anywhere

rise like a storm one night,
tear me away from the breast of a tree
and take me

desert mountain valley sea
anywhere... for once
where I feel not only
immured in a body

but a being that pulses
in the world's infinity

A Third History

With the hilt of a broken dagger in my hand
I think

      about daggers
      about hands that wield them
      about assassins and assaults
      about thousands of years in history

      and about a scream
      lost in some blind alley
      in a second suddenly…

(after a poem by Jorge Luis Borges)

गोलकुण्डा की एक शाम

(1)

...और ये बन्दोबस्त
ये नज़रिये
कहाँ-कहाँ से इकट्ठे हुए हौसले
कहाँ-कहाँ से इकट्ठे हुए शाही हुजूम
इन चढ़ाइयों
इन ढलानों पर
थरथराते घुटनों पर खड़ी इमारतें लुढ़कने-लुढ़कने को
बिना छत के कमरों दालानों में
मुश्किल से फ़र्क़ कर पातीं दीवारें
बहुत लम्बी बहुत मज़बूत चट्टानों में
उकाबी जांबाज़ों के उजाड़ घोंसले
और वो दिलेर उड़ानें...

इन बेतरतीब पंक्तियों को
किस तरकीब में सजायें कि 'शाबाश' गूंजे
पताकाओं की तरह लहराते शब्दों में—
कम वीरान लगें
वीराने?

(2)

थककर बैठ गया हूँ जिस जगह
ठीक इसी जगह एक शाही क़ैदी ने फ़ैसला किया था
कि क़ायम रहेंगी पत्थरों पर खरोंची हुई ये नक़्क़ाशियां

74

An Evening in Golconda[8]

(1)

...and these orchestrations
these points of view
brave-hearts gathered here from so many places
spectators of royalty from so many places
on these ascents
these difficult slopes
monuments standing on tremulous knees about to tumble down
walls that barely tell
roofless rooms from courtyards
on very long very strong crags
the derelict abodes of daredevils
and undaunted falcon flights...

With what craft shall we arrange
these dissonant lines
so that 'bravo' may echo
in words fluttering like flags—
so that these desolations
may look less desolate...

(2)

Right here, where I've sat down tired,
a royal prisoner had once resolved
that these etchings scratched out on mute rocks
shall persist

मेरी बेगुनाही का सबूत ये प्रार्थनाएँ...
मैं फिर आऊँगा फ़ैसला सुनने इन अर्ज़ियों पर।

यहीं कहीं अगर खोदा जाय
तो मिल सकती है किसी तावीज़ पर खुदी हुई एक तारीख़
जब पैदा हुआ होगा एक ख़ुशनसीब बादशाह
जब बड़ा हुआ होगा अपने साम्राज्य से भी बड़ा एक बादशाह
जब दुनिया को जीतने निकला होगा एक बादशाह
जब अपने और अपनों से हार गया होगा एक बादशाह,
जब घिरते हुए अँधेरों के ख़िलाफ़
एक ख़ुद्दार कुत्बशाही ने सिर उठाए रखा,
जब विश्वासघात के मलबे में डूबा एक पूरा साम्राज्य
मोतियों की एक शाही माला की तरह उठाकर
अबुलहसन ने डाल दिया होगा आज़मशाह के गले में,
जब इस शाही लाशघर से नहा धोकर
आख़िरी बार निकला होगा एक शाही जनाज़ा...

(3)

मुझे सोने दो अभी नज़दीक की आवाज़ों,
मुझमें शोर करो अभी दूर की ख़ामोशियों,
कोई साँस ले रहा है अभी मेरे फेफड़ों में।
इन बन्दूकों कटारों पर कसी हुई मुट्ठियाँ,
ये कमरबन्द : कोने खदरों में चमगादड़ों की तरह लटके साये :
क़िलों की दीवारों पर गोह की तरह चढ़ती फफूँद :
साज़िश के चेहरों से नक़ाब उतारते ख़ूनी हाथ :
मौत की रहमदिल घाटी में उतरती एक ठण्डी शाम।

these prayers, the proof of his innocence...
he shall return
to hear the verdict on these appeals.

If we dig around somewhere here
we may find some date engraved on an amulet
when a fortunate king was born
when a king grew bigger than his kingdom
when a king set out to conquer the world
when a king lost to himself and his own,
when a proud dynasty kept its head high
against the enveloping darkness,
when Abul Hasan put around the neck of Azam Shah
an entire empire sunk in the rubble of deceit
like a royal necklace of pearls,
when from this regal mortuary bathed and cleansed
a royal procession came out for the last time...

(3)

Let me sleep for now, you voices of the near,
wake up in me, you silences of the far,
someone is still breathing in my lungs.
Fists grip these guns and daggers,
these waistbands, shadows hang
like bats in nooks and clefts,
moss creeps up on forts like monitor lizards,
bloody hands take off masks
from faces of conspiracy,
a cold evening descends
on the merciful valley of death.

(4)

'अँधेरा होने से पहले ही घर लौटना है,'
वह बेहतर जानता है सैलानियों की ज़रूरतों को
जो टैक्सी चलाता,
जो रोज़ उन्हें खण्डहर दिखाकर घर पहुँचाता,
जिसकी कोई वाबस्तगी नहीं
पर्यटकों या खण्डहरों से : उसके लिए वक़्त
वह वक़्त है जो मीटर की रफ़्तार से
नग़ाद गुज़र रहा।

टैक्सी ड्राइवर रहमतअलीशाह
या गाइड मत्सराज के पूर्वजों के युद्धों से
कहीं ज़्यादा कठिन है
वर्तमान से उन दोनों की लड़ाई,
उससे पराजित न होने के उनके मन्सूबे...

बारूद में आग लगाने के इतिहासों से अलग
एक तीसरा इतिहास भी है
रहमतशाह की बीड़ियों और
मत्सराज की माचिस के बीच सुलहों का।

(4)

'Must return home before it turns dark,'
he who drives a taxi knows
the needs of tourists better,
he shows them the ruins and takes them back
each day, he who is indifferent
to tourists and ruins—for him time
is the time that passes
at the rapid pace of a meter.

Far more onerous
than the battles of the ancestors
of taxi driver Rahmat Ali Shah
or guide Matsa Raj
is the struggle of the two with today,
their resolve to stay undefeated...

Removed from the histories
        of battles and igniting explosives
there is also a third history
of reconciliations
between the bidis of Rahmat Ali Shah
and the matchsticks of Matsa Raj.

नीरो का संगीत-प्रेम

कहते हैं कि रोमन सम्राट नीरो
संगीत का प्रेमी था।

बेला बजाता था
और अपने को दुनिया का
बेजोड़ बेलाकार समझता था।

एक दिन उसके सिपाही
एक ऐसे गायक को पकड़ कर
उसके सामने लाए
जिसे लोग देश का
सबसे बड़ा गायक मानते थे

सिपाहियों ने भाले से
उसे कुरेदते हुए सम्राट के सामने गाने को कहा
लेकिन गायक इतना भयभीत था
कि उसके गले से आवाज़ ही न निकली

इस पर उसे यातना दी जाने लगी
और वह दर्द से चीख़ने लगा।
सम्राट को उसका चीख़ना सुरीला लगा,
अपनी बेला पर वह
ऐसा एक भी आर्तनाद कभी नहीं निकाल सका था।

हुक्म हुआ कि उसे क़ैद में रखा जाए
ताकि वह भाग न जाए,

Nero's Love of Music

They say, the Roman emperor Nero
was a lover of music. He played
the fiddle
and thought of himself as the world's
unmatched fiddle-player.

One day, his legionaries caught
and presented before him
a musician
whom people regarded
as the land's greatest singer.

Jabbing him with a spear
they bid him sing
before the emperor, but
the singer was so petrified
no sound escaped his throat

So they began torturing him
and he began wailing in pain.
The emperor found this melodious,
on his fiddle he'd never been able
to produce a single wail

like this. It was decreed
that the singer be kept in jail
so he doesn't run away,

और रोज़ उसे
उस समय नीरो के सामने लाकर
यातना दी जाए
जब वह अपनी बेला पर अभ्यास करता हो।

धीरे-धीरे गायक अपना गायन भूल गया,
उसे केवल रुदन याद रहा।

बादशाह को ख़ुश करने के लिए
उसके सिपाही गायक को
रोज़ नई-नई यातनाओं से तड़पाते...

कला और दर्द के बीच रिश्ते को
समझने का
नीरो का यह अपना तरीक़ा था!

and presented before Nero daily
to be tortured at the time
Nero played his fiddle. Slowly,

the singer forgot how to sing,
he only remembered how to cry

To please the king
his soldiers tormented the singer
in creative ways every day...

It was Nero's own novel way
of understanding
the relation between art and pain.

अतीत के गली कूचों में

शाही महलों से दूर
इतिहास के गली-कूचों में भटकती है
एक आवारा सनक
कि इन्हीं में कहीं रहते हैं आज भी
ग़ालिब और मीर,
कि हाथ में लिए लकुटिया
बीच बज़ार में खड़ा वह अधनंगा फ़क़ीर
        हो सकता है कबीर,
कि सीकरी से दूर
किसी नदी के घाट पर
        हो सकती है किसी
        तुलसी या सूर की कुटिया...

ऊँची-ऊँची अट्टालिकाओं
और लक़दक़ शहरों के ऊपर से
अचानक गुज़र जाता है
एक लश्कर
        हवाई जहाज की तेज़ी से

In the Lanes and Bylanes of the Past[9]

Far away from splendorous palaces
in the lanes and bylanes of history
still wanders a wayward whim

    that maybe somewhere here
    even today
        live Ghalib and Mir

        maybe the half-clad fakir
          standing mid-bazaar with a staff in hand
            could be Kabir

            maybe on a river bank
            away from mighty Sikri
            could be the humble abode
                of a Sur or Tulsi...

Above soaring skyscrapers
and gleaming done-up cities
a regiment of troops
suddenly flies past
    fast like an aircraft

भर्तृहरि की विरक्ति

'क्या मैं चूम सकता हूँ, पिंगला
उस हँसते उजाले को
जो तुम्हारे गुलाबी होठों पर खेल रहा?'

 'नहीं : वह तुम्हारे लिए नहीं।
 वह एक राजा के
 अस्तबल के दरोगा का यथार्थ है
 —तुम्हें खोजना होगा अपने लिए
 कोई दूसरा उजाला,
 कोई दूसरा अमरफल।'

प्रेम, जिसे समझती रही वह
एक कामुक नर की ज़रूरत
 किसी का सपना था...

जब भी टूटता
बड़े से बड़े प्रेम में
विश्वास का आधार,
 अरण्य हो जाता है
 एक विक्षुब्ध मन :
एक भ्रम टूटता—व्यक्ति नहीं—
कि एक चुम्बन के योग्य भी नहीं जो
किसी योग्य नहीं वह प्यार।

The Estrangement of Bhartrihari [10]

'Can I kiss, Pingala,
that jubilant light playing
on your incarnadine lips?'

    'No, it is not for you.
    It is for the keeper
    of a king's stables,
    it is his truth—
    you must find yourself
    some other light,
    some other fruit
    of eternal youth.'

Love, which she took to be
the need of a lustful man, was
    Bhartrihari's utopia...

Whenever the bedrock of trust
in the most stubborn of loves
    breaks, a distraught heart
    becomes a wilderness:
an illusion breaks—not a person—
that love not even worth
a kiss, is worth nothing.

रात घर से बाहर निकल कर
सिसकती हवाओं के ठंडे निःश्वास में
    एक राहत थी।

अब भी संभव है जी सकना
एक अन्य जीवन
जीने की अन्य शर्तों पर—
    कुछ अधिक उदास
    लेकिन कहीं कम क्रूर।

उन्हें नष्ट नहीं किया,
कर सकता था
पर उन्हें ले लेने दिया
जो उन्होंने चाहा...
और इस तरह बचा लिया अपने लिए
उस बहुमूल्य दुनिया को
जिसमें इतनी संभावनाएँ हैं,
पूरी प्रकृति से साझे का कारोबार
    जिसमें न संचय है न अपव्यय,
    न लाभ हानि का हिसाब,
    केवल ऋतुओं का आवागमन...

वियोग की भंगिमाएँ
वैराग्य का शृंगार बन जातीं
    जब अप्सराएँ बन कर घेरतीं उसे
    उसकी ही अतृप्त वासनाएँ।

कृतज्ञ हूँ प्रेम का
जिसने खुशियों से भी बड़ी
एक उदासी से भर दिया है जीवन

Coming out of home at night
in the wintry sigh of sobbing winds
there was relief.

One could still live
another life, on other terms—
         a little more disconsolate
         but far less cruel.

I did not destroy them
though I could, he thought,
but let them take what they wished...
and so saved for myself
a priceless world
of so many possibilities,
         in camaraderie with nature
         without hoarding or squandering,
         without gain or loss—with just
         the coming and going of seasons...

The dance of estrangement
becomes the adornment of an ascetic
         whenever his unsated desires
         enfold him like nymphs.

I am beholden
to the love that filled me
with a melancholy
even greater than bliss

उस प्रेम को बेहद जीना चाहता हूँ
    बेहद समय में
        बेहद जगह बना कर,
—लोगों और चीज़ों से
रिश्तों और नातों के हवाले
छोटी-छोटी सूचनाओं से विभक्त होकर नहीं
अलग हटकर
देखना चाहता हूँ संसार को

अकेले हँसना चाहता हूँ
अकेले अपने पर
इस तरह कि हँसते-हँसते आँसू आ जाएँ
और लगे कि एक ही बात है हँसना और रोना—
    एक ही मुद्रा के दो पहलू,
    एक तरफ़ एक सुंदर चेहरा
    दूसरी तरफ़ एक भूली-बिसरी तिथि...

चेतना को असीम करके देखता है भर्तृहरि
    जैसे पत्थर में एक मूर्ति को देखता है शिल्पी
    मूर्ति में एक आत्मा को देखता है कवि
    आत्मा में ब्रह्म को देखता है ऋषि...

    और न ब्रह्म की सीमा है
        न चेतना की ही...

I wish to live that love
immensely, in eternal time
        creating an eternal space—
not torn by people and things
or trifling news from kith and kin,
        standing aside
        I wish to watch the world

I wish to laugh alone
at myself alone,
go on laughing so that tears fill the eyes,
as if laughing and crying
were the same thing—
        two sides of the same coin,
        a beautiful face on one side
        on the other a forgotten date.

Making his sentience limitless
Bhartrihari sees
        like a sculptor sees a statue in stone,
        a poet sees a soul in a statue,
        a saint sees the universe in a soul...

        and neither the universe has a limit
                nor sentience...

विजयनगर

ऐतिहासिक भर होते हैं नगर
प्रागैतिहासिक होता है वन
नगर वह नागरिक प्रस्तावना
सभ्यताएँ जिसकी विजयों के क्षण।

प्रत्येक उद्यान के नीचे दबा होता
एक पराजित जंगल का मन
कभी-कभी वहीं से शुरू होता
एक नयी सभ्यता का व्याकरण।

एक बीज आक्रमण करता। सब से पहले
दिखाई देती उसकी बर्बर जीवन-शक्ति,
फिर एक ज़्यादा बड़े फ़लक पर
उसकी विजयों की सूक्ष्मतर अभिव्यक्ति।

यह हक्का बक्का नगर अब नगर नहीं
अपना ही अमूर्त अस्थि-पंजर है
यहीं कहीं वेदाचार्य सायण का घर भी था
जहाँ अब जलकुम्भी से ढका हुआ सरोवर है।

कभी कभी यों भी पनपती है हरियाली
कि भीतर ही भीतर सूख जाते तालाब,
ऊपर की जिल्द तो हरी भरी लगती है
दीमकें चाट जाती हैं अन्दर की किताब।

Vijayanagar, The City of Victory[11]

Cities are only historic
but forests are primeval,
civilisations are the final triumphs
of cities begun by people.

Under every garden is buried
the heart of a defeated jungle,
the grammar of a new civilisation
begins at times from there as well.

A seed invades—first of all is seen
its ravenous life energy,
then on a larger horizon
the subtler vistas of its victory.

This Hakka-Bukka city is now no more
than its own shapeless skeleton,
somewhere here lived Sayan where now
is a pond draped in hyacinth.

Sometimes foliage flourishes so
that ponds dry up from deep within,
the outer covers look lush and green,
termites consume the book therein.

'बाज़ार अनारकली', लाहौर
—एक शाम

उस शाम कुछ ज़्यादा ही
गुलज़ार लगा था 'बाज़ार अनारकली'
कुछ ज़्यादा बेचैन हो उठी थी
इतिहास की एक भूली-बिसरी गली

एक उदास शाहज़ादा
ठहरा कर बादलों का लश्कर
उतरता एक सफ़ेद घोड़े से
और एक मामूली-सी दीवार के
झरोखे में रख देता एक जलता चिराग़

दीवार में चुनी
कसमसाती एक प्रेम की कहानी
जैसे कोई फ़रियाद
आज भी ज़िन्दा
एक बेदम आवाज़ से पुकारे

एक छाया
दूसरी से गले मिलती
—एक हिंसा
प्रथा में आततायी
उन्हें फिर से अलग करती

'Bazaar Anarkali', Lahore
—A Twilight [12]

That evening, Bazaar Anarkali
had looked festive
somewhat more than usual

A forgotten lane of history
had grown restive
more so than usual…

A heavy-hearted prince
pauses a battalion of clouds,
dismounts from a white stallion,
and places a lighted lamp
in the alcove of a nondescript wall

Entombed inside the wall
a floundering tale of love
like some beseechment
still alive today
calls out in a feeble voice

A shadow
embraces another to its breast,
a savagery
tyrannical by tradition
severs them from each other again…

गुज़रती बीते दिनों की कुछ यादें
मीनारों के सहारे
डूब जाता एक ख़्वाब
डूबते सूरज के किनारे

छलक आते
अँधेरों की बर्दाश्त के बाहर
तारे... और तारे...

Rememories of bygone days stream past
holding on to minarets
a dream drowns
alongside the setting sun

Beyond the endurance of so many nightfalls
the eyes of a sky well up
    and spill out stars...
        still more stars

वे जो नहीं जानते

एक ठोकर लगी
तो ठोकर-बराबर चोट लगी माथे पर
खून छलक आया
तो आँखें भर आईं

माथे ने डाँटा,
'तुम चुप रहो,
तुमसे क्या मतलब?'

ठोकर ने कहा, 'सॉरी...'
और आगे बढ़ गई
गुज़रते ज़माने की तेज़ रफ्तार से।

एक बूढ़े का आहत आत्मसम्मान
लाठी टेके
कहीं छूट गया युगों पीछे

मुड़कर देखा पीछे
वह कुछ पहचाना-सा लगा।
पूछा उससे, 'कौन हो तुम?'
सिर ऊँचा करके उसने कहा, 'गाँधी!'

मैं चौंका—'लेकिन तुम तो मारे जा चुके हो, बापू!'
'नहीं,' उन्होंने दृढ़ता से कहा,
'मैं हर समय मौजूद हूँ
एक ऐसा रास्ता जिस पर चलकर
दुनिया की किसी भी अत्याचारी स्थिति से
पाई जा सकती है आज़ादी।'

Those Who Do Not Know

A blow, so the head was hurt
    Some blood spilled
    So tears filled the eyes.

    The head reprimanded,
    'You keep quiet,
    How does it concern you?'

The blow said, 'Sorry…' and moved on
    At the fast pace of the passing times.

An old man's injured dignity
Propped up on a stick
Was left somewhere epochs behind.

I turned back to look, he looked
A bit familiar. I asked,
'Who are you?' He raised his head high
    And said, 'Gandhi.'

I was taken aback—'But you've been killed, Bapu?'
    'No,' he said resolutely,
    'I am present all the time,
    A path, which can always be walked
    And freedom found
    From any injustice, any oppressive
    Condition of the world.'

चन्द्रगुप्त मौर्य

अब सुलह कर लो
उस पारदर्शी दुश्मन की सीमाहीनता से
जिसने तुम्हें
तुम्हारे ही गढ़ में घेर लिया है

कहाँ तक लड़ोगे
ऐश्वर्य की उस धंसती हुई
विवादास्पद ज़मीन के लिए
जो तुम्हारे पाँवों के नीचे से खिसक रही?

अपनी स्वायत्तता के अधिकारों को त्यागते ही
तुम्हारे शरीर पर जकड़ी जंज़ीरें
शिथिल पड़ जायेंगी। तुम अनुभव करोगे
एक अजीब-सा हल्कापन।
उस शक्ति-अधिग्रहण को स्वीकार करते ही
तुम्हें प्रदान किया जाएगा
मैत्री का एक ढीला चोला

एक कुशा-मुकुट
सहारे के लिए एक काष्ठ-कोदंड
और तुम्हारे ही साम्राज्य में दूर कहीं
एक छोटा-सा क़िला
जिसके अन्दर ही अन्दर तुम
धीरे-धीरे इस संसार से विरक्त होते चले जाओगे

The Last Days of
Chandragupta Maurya[13]

Make peace now
with the infinity of that transparent enemy
who has besieged you
in the stronghold of your own citadel...

How long will you cross swords
for that disputed ground of glory
fast sinking and slipping away
from under your feet?

As soon as you relinquish
your right to reign,
the fetters on your body will loosen
and give way, you will feel
a strange sort of lightness

As soon as you accept
that other power, you will be granted
a loose cloak of friendship
a laurel coronet
a wooden longbow for support
and somewhere far in your own kingdom
a small abode
deep within which you will slowly go on
getting detached from this world

तुम्हारा पुनर्जन्म होगा सदियों बाद
किसी अनुश्रुति में एक शिलालेख के रूप में

अबकी वर्तमान में नहीं, अतीत में—
जहाँ तुम विदग्ध सम्राटों की सूची में
स्वयं को अंकित पाओगे।

You will be reborn centuries later
in some legend in an epitaph

this time not in the present
but in the past—
and there you will find yourself inscribed
in the chronicle of far-sighted kings.

this time not in the present
but in the past

I Reached This World
a Little Late

With new spectacles on my eyes
I can see better now
With new machines on my ears
I can hear better now...

Now
I only wish
to see and hear
a better world

असमंजस

हो सकता है यह आज का नहीं
मुझसे बहुत पहले का कोई समय हो

और जहाँ हमें पहुँचना है कल
वहाँ छोटे-छोटे बच्चे
उत्सुकता से प्रतीक्षा कर रहे हों
कि देखें उनके लिए
क्या लेकर आता है मेरा युग

एक हाथ में लिए आज का अख़बार
दूसरे में कविताएँ
        असमंजस में हूँ
        कि पहले उन्हें ख़बरें सुनाऊँ
        या कविताएँ...

Hesitation

It is possible that this is not
a time of today
but of sometime long before us

and there
where we must reach tomorrow
little children are waiting for us
with bated breath
to see what our epoch
brings for them after all...

With today's newspaper in one hand
and poems in the other
    I hesitate

      should I first read to them the news
      or the poems...

ज़रा देर से इस दुनिया में

मैं ज़रा देर से इस दुनिया में पहुँचा

तब तक पूरी दुनिया
सभ्य हो चुकी थी

सारे जंगल काटे जा चुके थे
जानवर मारे जा चुके थे
वर्षा थम चुकी थी
और तप रही थी पृथ्वी
आग के गोले की तरह...

चारों तरफ़ लोहे और कंक्रीट के
बड़े-बड़े घने जंगल उग आये थे
जिनमें दिखायी दे रहे थे
आदमी का ही शिकार करते कुछ आदमी
अत्यन्त विकसित तरीक़ों से...

मैं ज़रा देर से इस दुनिया में पहुँचा

A Little Late in This World

I reached this world a little late

By then the whole globe
had been civilised

All forests had been felled
animals had been slain
the rain had ceased
and the whole earth was simmering
      like an infernal orb of blaze…

On all sides dense gigantic jungles
of iron and concrete had arisen
and in them could be seen some
people preying on other people
      in the most modern and evolved of ways…

I reached this world a little late

बर्बरों का आगमन

कवाफ़ी की कविता 'बर्बरों की प्रतीक्षा' से सन्दर्भ लेकर

अब किसी भी बात को लेकर
चिन्ता करना व्यर्थ है। वे आ गये हैं। उन्होंने
फिर एक बार हमें जीत लिया है।

उनके अफ़सर, सिपाही और कोतवाल—
उनके सलाहकार, मसख़रे और नक़्क़ाल—
उनके दरबारी और उनके नमकहलाल—
उनके मुसाहिब, ख़ुशामदी और दलाल—
चारों तरफ़
छा गये हैं। वे सब के सब
वापस आ गये हैं।

शहर की सभी ख़ास और आम जगहों पर उनका कब्ज़ा है।
उनके जत्थे अब
लूट की खुली छूट के लिए बेताब हैं।

Arrival of the Barbarians

After Cavafy's 'Waiting for the Barbarians'

It is no use fretting about anything
Now. They have arrived. Once again
They have trounced and conquered us.

Their officers, constables and brigadiers
Counsellors, bailiffs, henchmen and jesters
Pimps, sycophants, jobbers and soothsayers
Their lackeys, marshals and their courtiers—

They are there, shadowing us
Everywhere. All of them
Have come back, again

They have taken over all the common
And prime places in the city all over.

Their mobs are now raring
For a free hand to maraud.

फिर मेरे पाँवों तले

फिर मेरे पाँवों तले
रख दी गई है एक पृथ्वी

फिर मुझे थमा दी गई है
एक ज़िन्दगी की लगाम

थरथराते पाँवों में
फंसा दी गई हैं रक़ाबें

फिर उठता चारों ओर
वही पागल शोर
नसों पर फिर वही असह्य दबाव
        'या तो सिद्ध करो दिग्विजय
        या स्वीकार करो दास-भाव।'

फिर मुझे लड़ना है वही पुराना युद्ध
उसी नक़ाबपोश दुश्मन के विरुद्ध
        जिसकी फ़ौजें
        छिपकर अँधेरे में वार करतीं।

भारी मन से फिर मुझे लौटना है
        उसी कुरुक्षेत्र—उसी पानीपत—उसी प्लासी के
        रक्त-सने धूसर मैदानों से
        एक थके हुए योद्धा की तरह ख़ाली हाथ।

A World Under My Feet

An earth has been placed under
my feet again

The reins of a life have been put
in my hands again

Stirrups have been tethered
on tremulous feet

The same corybantic din
crescendoes all around again
in every jaded nerve
the same frenetic strain—
       prove supreme victory, or
       accept the yoke of servility

Again, I must fight the same old battle
against the same masked adversary
whose armies strike covertly, in the dark

Again, return I must
with a heavy heart
from the dusty blood-sodden fields
of the same Kurukshetra—
       the same Panipat—the same Plassey
like a worn-out trooper, empty-handed

महासच

निकला तो था
एक छोटे से सच की तलाश में
कि रास्ते में मिल गया
एक महासच।
घबराकर गिर पड़ा उसके चरणों में
और गिड़गिड़ाया—बचाओ, बचाओ
हमारे बच्चों बराबर
छोटे-छोटे सचों की जान ख़तरे में है।

उसने आश्वस्त किया—घबराओ मत
अब सच को खोजने
तुम्हें मन वन में नहीं जाना होगा
वह तुम्हें खोज लेगा कहीं भी
तमाम माध्यमों के द्वारा सीधे
तुम्हारे घर में प्रवेश करेगा, तुम्हारे बच्चों के
साथ खेलेगा और उन्हीं के साथ बड़ा होगा इस तरह
कि उसके सामने
पूरी दुनिया छोटी पड़ जाएगी
एक बहुत बड़ी मशीन की तरह
होगा वह सच—
तमाम चलते पुरजों का संग्रह!

तब से बच्चों बराबर
छोटे-छोटे सच तो अन्तर्ध्यान हैं
और उनकी जगह
एक-से-एक-बड़े-महासच
अपने विकराल रूपों में वर्तमान हैं।

Mega Truth

Well, he had started out
to seek a little truth
but found en route
a mega truth.
Panicking, he fell at its feet
and cringed—help, help
the endangered lives of our
tiny child-sized truths.

Do not panic—it assured.
Now, to find truth you'll
not need a mind or idyll,
it'll find you anywhere
using myriad means, it'll enter
your home straight away, it'll play
with your children and grow up
with them, in front of it
the whole world will feel small.
That truth will be
a giant machine, an assembly
of countless circling cogs.

Since then, small childlike truths
have waned into oblivion
and in their place mega truths,
one mightier than the other,
are today of monstrous mien.

आँकड़ों की बीमारी

एक बार मुझे आँकड़ों की उल्टियाँ होने लगीं
गिनते गिनते जब संख्या
करोड़ों को पार करने लगी
मैं बेहोश हो गया

होश आया तो मैं अस्पताल में था
ख़ून चढ़ाया जा रहा था
ऑक्सीजन दी जा रही थी
कि मैं चिल्लाया

डॉक्टर मुझे बुरी तरह हँसी आ रही
यह हँसानेवाली गैस है शायद
प्राण बचानेवाली नहीं
तुम मुझे हँसने पर मजबूर नहीं कर सकते
इस देश में हर एक को अफ़सोस के साथ जीने का
पैदाइशी हक़ है वरना
कोई माने नहीं रखते हमारी आज़ादी और प्रजातंत्र

बोलिए नहीं—नर्स ने कहा—बेहद कमज़ोर हैं आप
बड़ी मुश्किल से क़ाबू में आया है रक्तचाप
डॉक्टर ने समझाया—आँकड़ों का वाइरस
बुरी तरह फैल रहा आजकल
सीधे दिमाग़ पर असर करता
भाग्यवान हैं आप कि बच गए
कुछ भी हो सकता था आपको—

The Pandemic of Numbers

He once began to vomit up numbers
uncontrollably, counting,
when the toll began to cross millions
he slipped into a coma, then

woke up in a hospital where blood was
being transfused, oxygen was being given…
that he screamed out—

Doctor, I'm bursting with laughter,
this is laughing gas, not life-saving gas,
you can't compel me to laugh
in this country, all have a birthright
to live in remorse, else what's the meaning
of our freedom, democracy, republic…

Don't talk, said the nurse, you're weak,
it was a feat to control your blood pressure,
the doctor explained—this virus of numbers
is unfurling like wildfire these days,
it affects the brain straightaway,
you're fortunate to have been saved,
anything could've happened to you—

सन्निपात कि आप बोलते ही चले जाते
या पक्षाघात कि हमेशा के लिए बन्द हो जाता
आपका बोलना
मस्तिष्क की कोई भी नस फट सकती थी
इतनी बड़ी संख्या के दबाव से

हम सब एक नाज़ुक दौर से गुज़र रहे
तादाद के मामले में उत्तेजना घातक हो सकती है
आँकड़ों पर कोई दवा काम नहीं करती
शान्ति से काम लें
अगर बच गए आप तो करोड़ों में एक होंगे...

अचानक मुझे लगा
ख़तरों से सावधान कराते किसी संकेत-चिह्न में
बदल गई थी डॉक्टर की सूरत
और मैं आँकड़ों का काटा
चीख़ता चला जा रहा था
कि हम आँकड़े नहीं आदमी हैं

Delirium, and you would've gone on blathering,
or paralysis, and you could've ceased
talking forever,
any vein in your head could've ruptured
under pressure from such a titanic count:
we're passing through friable times,
excitement over data can be fatal,
no medicines work on numbers.
Stay calm,
if you're saved, you'd be one in a million...

Suddenly he felt
the doctor's face had transformed
into a red alert, warning
against some imminent danger.
And he, lacerated by numbers,
was screaming away—we are
people even now, not numbers...

वर्षफल

जब से सुना है
कि सितारे भी शामिल हैं
हमारी क़िस्मतों के खेल में
कुछ मज़ा-सा आने लगा है
खेलने में यह खेल जिसमें
सारे सितारे उस तरफ़
और मैं अकेला इस तरफ़...

कुछ है इस एकतरफ़ा स्थिति में ही
जिसमें मेरी जीत है।

जानता हूँ मारा जाऊँगा
किन्तु हारूँगा नहीं।

खेलने यही खेल
चुकाने जन्म-जन्मांतरों का हिसाब

खोजता हुआ आऊँगा उसी बिरहमन को
जिसने ग़ालिब को बताया था
कि ये साल अच्छा है।

Horoscope for the Year[14]

Since the time I heard that
stars are also embroiled
in the game of our destinies
    it has been somewhat enticing
    to play this game where
            all the stars are on that side
            and I am alone on this side.

Something in this one-sidedness
itself points to my triumph.

    I know I may be killed, but I will
    not concede defeat—

To play this game
and settle the accounts of life after life

    I will again come looking
    for that same Birahaman
    who had once told Ghalib
    that this year will be good.

ताबूत की सुन्दरी

सैकड़ों साल पुराने
एक ताबूत को किताब की तरह खोला

आँखें मलती हुई उठ बैठी एक सुन्दरी

वही प्राचीन चेहरा
            जाना पहचाना

देख कर मैं चौंक पड़ा! मैंने पूछा—
'तुम, और इस ताबूत में?'

उसने कहा—'यह ताबूत नहीं
        टी. वी. है। और मेरी कहानी
        गतांक से आगे का वृत्तान्त…'

ऐसा कह कर उसने एक जम्हाई ली
और फिर ताबूत में लेट गई।

उसके लेटते ही
ताबूत एक करवट ले कर खड़ा हो गया
किसी मकान के सदर दरवाज़े की तरह :

दरवाज़ा खोल कर वही पुरानी कहानी
बनी-ठनी बाहर निकली कुछ इस अन्दाज़ से
मानो वह बिल्कुल नयी हो,
और उसकी अपेक्षा अपने को दुहराती दुनिया   पुरानी

Belle of the Coffin

Opening a million-year-old
coffin like a book
a beauty sat up in it
rubbing her eyes

The same antiquated face
       hackneyed, familiar

It was a shock to see her—
'You, and in this coffin?'

'This isn't a coffin,' she said.
       'It's a TV. And my serial story
       from after the last episode...'

Saying this, she yawned
and lay down in the coffin again.

As soon as she did
the coffin turned once, then stood up
like the front door to a house:

Unbolting the door, that same old story again
sashayed out all primped up, her mien bold,
as if she were spanking new, and relative to her
the world, repeating itself,   the same old.

घुड़सवार

निकलकर बाहर आना चाहता हूँ
उस पहली पाठ्य-पुस्तक से
जिसके मुखपृष्ठ पर
एक पुराना ज़माना
हाथ में लिये नंगी तलवार
एक घोड़े पर मुस्तैदी से सवार है
अभी तक

प्रवेश करना चाहता हूँ
किसी ऐसी सदी में
जिसकी सदियों से प्रतीक्षा है

सड़कों और गलियों में
आमने-सामने क़तार से लगे मकान
जैसे किसी लाइब्रेरी में लगी किताबें

सुबह सुबह हर मकान का दरवाज़ा
खुलता जैसे खुलती है एक नयी किताब

निकलता है उसमें से
आज का एक आदमी

लेकिन उसी तरह घोड़े पर सवार
दिन भर अपना घोड़ा दौड़ाता

Horsemen

One wishes to step out
Of that first textbook
On whose first page
A bygone age
With a bared sabre in hand
Is haughtily mounted on horseback
Even today

One wishes to enter some century
For which we have been
Waiting for centuries

In streets and alleys
Houses are queued up facing each other
Like books queued up in libraries

Daily at daybreak
The door of each house
Opens like a new book

And from it comes out
A man of today…

But mounted on horseback
In the same old way
He canters his horse around
The whole, long day

ईश्वर साक्षी है

जन्म लेते ही हमने शपथ ली थी
ईश्वर को साक्षी बनाकर
कि हम लड़ेंगे नहीं—
    क्यों कि हम
    पिता-पुत्र हैं
    भाई-भाई हैं
    नाते-रिश्तेदार हैं
    दोस्त और प्रियजन हैं।

फिर हमने शपथ ली
लड़ाई के मैदान में
ईश्वर को साक्षी बनाकर
कि हम में से कोई पीछे नहीं हटेगा—
    क्यों कि यहाँ कोई किसी का सगा नहीं
    सब एक दूसरे के दुश्मन हैं
    सब की अपनी अपनी लड़ाई है।

लड़ाई आज भी जारी है
लोग आज भी लड़ मर रहे हैं

ईश्वर साक्षी है।

God is Our Witness

We took an oath at birth
making God our witness
that we will never fight—
    because we are
    brother and brother
    father and son
    kith and kin
    friend, dear one.

Then we took an oath
in the field of battle
making God our witness
that none of us will step back—
    for here no one is anyone's own
    all are each other's rivals
    all have their own battles.

Even today, the battles rage on
People continue to fight and die, unknown

God is the witness.

जितना ही ख़ुश रखना चाहता हूँ

दाभोलकर, पानसरे और कलबुर्गी की हत्या के बाद

जितना ही ख़ुश रखना चाहता हूँ
उतनी ही उदास होती जाती हैं मेरी कविताएँ
विह्वल प्रार्थनाओं में बदल जाते हैं शब्द

बीहड़ रेगिस्तानों में
बंजारों की तरह भटकते
या काल्पनिक अभयारण्य में
शरण पाना चाहते हैं वे

जितना हम चाहते हैं बड़ा फ़ासला बना रहे
अत्याचारी और निर्दोष जन के बीच
उतना ही भयानक होता जाता
हमारे समय का सच

नृशंस हत्याओं का रक्त
जल्दी सूखने से इनकार करता
उसकी चिनगारियाँ दूर तक पहुँचतीं

हमें आक्रांत करता
एक आदिम अँधेरा
होता जाता है गहरा
और गहरा

The Happier I Wish to Keep Them

After the killings of Dabholkar, Pansare and Kalburgi

The more I wish to keep them happy
The more forlorn my poems become

Words turn into fevered prayers
On their own

They drift about like nomads
In the wastelands of deserts
Or seek haven in the imagined
Sanctuary of woodlands

The stronger we yearn for a distance to remain
Between innocence and tyranny
The more fiendish the truth of our time
Grows to be

The blood of barbaric murder
Refuses to dry up

Its ripples draw out far

Beleaguering all of us...
A primal, cavernous nightfall
Sinks in deeper

Still deeper

शब्द जो खो जाते हैं

हमारी भाषा की सीमाएँ हमारे संसार की सीमाएँ हैं
—विट्गेनश्टाइन

कुछ शब्द हैं
जो अपमानित होने पर
स्वयं ही जीवन और भाषा से
बाहर चले जाते हैं।

'पवित्रता' ऐसा ही एक शब्द है
जो अब व्यवहार में नहीं,
उसकी जाति के शब्द
अब ढूँढे नहीं मिलते
हवा पानी मिट्टी तक में।

ऐसा कोई जीता जागता उदाहरण
दिखायी नहीं देता आजकल
जो सिद्ध और प्रमाणित कर सके
उस शब्द की शत-प्रतिशत शुद्धता।

ऐसा ही एक शब्द था 'शान्ति'।
अब विलुप्त हो चुका उसका वंश,
कहीं नहीं दिखायी देती वह
न किसी के अन्दर न बाहर,
कहते हैं मृत्यु के बाद वह मिलती है।

मुझे शक होता है
ऐसी हर चीज़ पर
जो मृत्यु के बाद मिलती है।

Words that Disappear

The limits of my language are the limits of my world
—Wittgenstein

There are some words
that if abased
leave life and language
of their own accord.

'Purity' is one word
not in vogue any more,
words of its kind are hard to find
even inside
water soil or air

No such living instance
these days can attest
to its unblemished innocence.

Another word was 'peace',
its halcyon clan is extinct
now, it is nowhere to be seen
within or without

They say one finds it after death,
but I am suspicious
of all things found after death.

शायद 'प्रेम' भी ऐसा ही एक शब्द है
जिसकी अब यादें भर बची हैं
भाषा में।

ज़िन्दगी से पलायन करते जा रहे हैं
ऐसे तमाम तिरस्कृत शब्द
जो कभी उसका गौरव थे।

वे कहाँ चले जाते हैं
हमारी दुनिया को छोड़ने के बाद।

शायद वे एकान्तवासी हो जाते हैं
और अपने को इतना अकेला कर लेते हैं
कि फिर कोई भाषा उन तक पहुँच नहीं पाती।

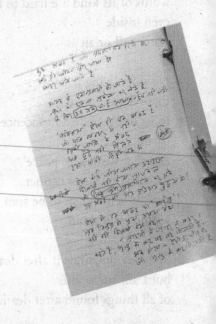

Perhaps 'love' is also such a word
whose mere remembrance
clings to language now.

Countless such cast-off
words, once the pride of life,
keep getting exiled...

Where do they go
after leaving our world

Perhaps they turn into hermits
and make themselves so infinitely solitary
that then no language is able
to reach them again.

Of Another Time,
Another Place

Some want everything some nothing
between two paradoxes
under the open sky in open fields
a homeless gypsy wanders carefree...

in his world
the margins don't move
the roads run

in his day
everything is now,
in itself, nearby... nothing to run after

अंकोर वाट

वट वृक्ष से नीचे
ख़ामोश उतरती हैं जड़ें
विह्वल आत्माएँ

मन्दिरों के महावन में
प्रवेश करती हैं
हाथ जोड़े प्रार्थी जड़ें

पत्तियों के मर्मर में गूँजती हैं दीक्षाएँ
सुदूर प्रार्थनाएँ

मंद हवाओं में झूमते हैं मन्दिर
शिलाओं का शिल्प हो गयी हैं शाखाएँ
शाखाओं की कोमलता हो गयी हैं शिलाएँ
दोनों एक परमत्व में तन्मय
          सदियों से समाधिस्थ
          वट वृक्ष तले
          ध्यानमग्न बोधिसत्त्व

किसी पोल पोट के नृशंस यथार्थ के विरुद्ध
कलाओं का शान्तिवन
          रचता
          महाकरुणा का अतियथार्थ

Angkor Wat

down the banyan tree
roots descend silently
disquiet souls

in the vast forest of temples
devotee roots
enter with folded hands

incantations echo in the rustle of leaves
distant supplications

temples sway in the slow air
branches become the sculpture of rocks
rocks the gentle body of branches
both one in sempiternity
        in a meditative trance for centuries
        beneath the banyan tree
        a bodhisattva in contemplation

against some Pol Pot's reality
the forest of art and tranquillity
        begets
        a surreality of supreme compassion

नाज़िम हिकमत के साथ, 1955

वे मॉस्को से वॉरसॉ आए थे
तुर्की के कठोर जेल-जीवन की थकान
अभी ताज़ा थी उनके चेहरे पर।

याद आता एक रेस्त्रां
किसी गिरजाघर के नज़दीक जो अब
एक रहस्य की तरह चुप है,
लेखकों का जमावड़ा
जहाँ पहली बार और फिर कई बार
हिकमत से मिला था।

याद हैं उनके भारी, खुरदुरे, किसानी हाथ
मेरे घुटनों पर—हाथों पर—
जब वे उत्साहित होकर
समझाते थे कोई बात...

सारी बातें याद नहीं
लेकिन अच्छी तरह याद है
एक कवि का व्यक्तित्व
जिसने अपनी अदम्य जिजीविषा से
भर दिया था कभी
एक कवि का शुरुआती जीवन।

वक़्त बदलता—दृश्य बदलते—जगहें बदलतीं
लेकिन बहुत नहीं बदलतीं
एक कवि होने की वजहें
        उसकी चिंताएँ,
किसी अधूरी-सी भेंट की याद
        जीवन को अधिक संपूर्ण बनाती हुई।

With Nazim Hikmet, 1955

He had come from Moscow to Warsaw,
the fatigue of Turkey's harsh prison-life
still alive on his face. I remember

a restaurant, near a church that is now
mute like a mystery,
a congregation of fervid writers
where for the first time, and then
many a time, I met Hikmet. I remember

his heavy, coarse, rustic hands
on my hands, on my knees,
when he made a spirited point to me…

I do not remember all his words
but I do remember a poet
in that onerous time,
an unflinching will to live
with which he filled
a poet's early years.

Times change, views and places change,
but a poet's reasons,
        the solicitudes,
do not change so much

the remembrances of some unfinished days
        enrich ever more,
        reassure.

पाब्लो नेरुदा से एक भेंट, वॉरसॉ 1955

ध्यान से देख रहा हूँ
वॉरसॉ के ब्रिस्टल होटल में उस जगह को
जो अब पचास वर्षों बाद
बिल्कुल बदल गई है।

तब वह होटल
एक तबाह नगर का
बचा-खुचा वैभव था।

सामने कुर्सी पर बैठा
चाय पी रहा वह व्यक्ति
कहीं वही तो नहीं?

हिम्मत की, पास जाकर हिचकते हुए पूछा—
'आप वही तो नहीं
जो चाहता है कि पूरी पृथ्वी
एक आवास हो सबका
जिसमें हर कोई रह सके
सकुशल और निश्शंक?'

एक दबी मुस्कान से
चमक उठा था नेरुदा का चेहरा—
'बैठो, एक प्याला चाय पियो मेरे साथ :
क्या करते हो? कौन हो? कहाँ रहते हो?'
'पढ़ता लिखता हूँ,
भारतीय हूँ।'

Meeting Pablo Neruda, Warsaw 1955

I look intently
at that spot in Warsaw's Bristol Hotel
now completely changed
after fifty years

That hotel then
was the remnant glory
of a devastated city.

Sitting there on a chair
that person drinking tea
could he not perhaps be...

I go near and hesitantly ask—
    'Are you not perhaps he
    who wants the whole earth to be
    a residence for all,
    where all can live safely
    free from unease?'

Neruda's face had brightened—
    'Sit, have tea with me,
    what do you do, where do you live?'
'I write,
I'm from India...'

कुछ देर के लिए वे
डूब गए थे अपने में।
क्या सोच रहे थे वे—
फ़क़ीर दार्शनिकों का देश?
बोले, 'ओह, गांधी का देश।'

हमारे बीच एक मेज़ थी
और चाय के दो प्याले
बहुत-सी बातें हुईं...

उन्हें घर लौटने के लिए
एक उड़ान पकड़नी थी।

भारत लौटते हुए
एक उड़ान की ऊँचाई से
देख रहा था मैं भी
नीचे बिछी पृथ्वी पर छोटे-छोटे घरों को,
दूर-दूर तक फैले
एक-से यथार्थ को।

मैं नेरुदा से मिला था
आधी सदी पहले
एक युद्धाहत नगर में
जो तेज़ी से लौट रहा था
जीवन की ओर।

For a while, he
was a million miles away,
    what was he thinking—
    the country of philosophers and fakirs?
    'Oh, the country of Gandhi,' he said.

There was a table between us
and two cups,
    we spoke for long…
    then he had to take a flight
    to return home.

Returning to India
I could also see
from the height of a flight
a congeries of tiny houses on the earth beneath,
spread far and wide
    kindred realities

Half a century ago
at a delicate cusp, I had met Neruda
in a war-ravaged city
    fast returning
        towards life…

ट्यूनीशिया का कुआँ

ट्यूनीशिया में एक कुआँ है
कहते हैं उसका पानी
धरती के अन्दर ही अन्दर
उस पवित्र कुएँ से जुड़ा है
जो मक्का में है।

मैंने तो यह भी सुना है
कि धरती के अन्दर ही अन्दर
हर कुएँ का पानी
हर कुएँ से जुड़ा है।

A Well in Tunisia

There is a well in Tunisia
whose water, it is said,
deep down inside the earth
    unites
        with that sacred well
        in Mecca

In fact, I have even heard that
deep down inside the earth
the water of every well
    unites
        with every well
        everywhere

एक चीनी कविमित्र द्वारा बनाए
अपने एक रेखाचित्र को सोचते हुए

यह मेरे एक चीनी कविमित्र का
झटपट बनाया हुआ रेखाचित्र है

मुझे नहीं मालूम था कि मैं
रेखांकित किया जा रहा हूँ

मैं कुछ सुन रहा था
कुछ देख रहा था
कुछ सोच रहा था

उसी समय में
रेखाओं के माध्यम से
मुझे भी कोई
देख, सुन और सोच रहा था :
रेखाओं में एक कौतुक है
जिससे एक काराज़ी व्योम खेल रहा है

उसमें कल्पना का रंग भरते ही
चित्र बदल जाता है
किसी अनाम याली की
ऊबड़-खाबड़ याताओं में

शायद मैं विभिन्न देशों को जोड़ने वाले
किसी 'रेशम-मार्ग' पर भटक रहा था

Contemplating a Sketch of Me
Made by a Chinese Poet-Friend [15]

This is a hurriedly made sketch
by a Chinese poet-friend

I did not know
I was being drawn

> I was seeing something
> hearing, thinking something

At the same time,
through the measure of lines, someone was
        seeing, hearing and thinking me:

There is a levity in lines
playing with the paper's void

When the colour of imagination fills it
the whole picture at once
transforms into
the rough and rugged travels of
        a nameless traveller

Perhaps, I was roving about
on some silk road
        stringing nations together

ऐतिहासिक फ़ासले

अच्छी तरह याद है
तब तेरह दिन लगे थे ट्रेन से
साइबेरिया के मैदानों को पार करके
मॉस्को से बीजिंग तक पहुँचने में।

अब केवल सात दिन लगते हैं
उसी फ़ासले को तय करने में—
हवाई-जहाज़ से सात घंटे भी नहीं लगते।

पुराने ज़मानों में बरसों लगते थे
उसी दूरी को तय करने में।

दूरियों का भूगोल नहीं
उनका समय बदलता है।

कितना ऐतिहासिक लगता है आज
तुमसे मिलना उस दिन!

Historic Separations
For the mysterious Olga

I remember well, it took thirteen days by train then
to cross the fields of Siberia from Moscow to Beijing.

It takes less than seven days
to cover the same separation now—
    doesn't even take
    seven hours by air.

In ancient times
it would have taken years to traverse the same distance.

It is not the geography of distances
    but their time
        that transforms.

How historic it seems today
to have met you on that day.

द्वारिका में सुदामा

किस मायानगरी में
भटक रहे हो सुदामा?
    यह द्वारिका तो दिल्ली का
    एक छोटा-सा मुहल्ला है!
    यहाँ ऐसा कोई नहीं
    जो तुम्हें जानता हो।

जिसे तुम खोज रहे
वह अब इस दुनिया में नहीं
किसी और दुनिया में रहता है
जिसका कोई पता ठिकाना नहीं :
    उसकी नगरी कहीं डूब चुकी है
    समुद्र की तलहटी में,
    और उसके महलों में अब
    मछलियाँ विहार करती हैं।

क्या भेंट लाए हो अपने गाँव से
उसके लिए? मुट्ठी भर चावल?
    एक ठहाका लगाता है द्वारपाल—
    ये तो मेरी बख़्शिश के लिए भी काफ़ी नहीं!

कैसी बाँसुरी? कैसा नाच? कौन गिरधारी?
    जिस महल को तुम
    भौचक खड़े देख रहे
    वह तो उसका है
    जिसकी कमर की लचकों में
    हीरों की खान है!

Sudama in Dwarika[16]

In what city of illusions are you
Wandering wildered, Sudama?
    This Dwarika is only
    A little suburb of Delhi.
    There is no one here
    Who knows you.

The one you're looking for doesn't
Dwell in this world now
But in some other world
No one knows about
    His city has sunk somewhere
    To some ground beneath the sea
    And in his palaces now
    Fish frolic about.

What gift did you bring from your village
For him? A handful of rice?
    The door-keeper guffaws—
    This won't even make for my tip.

What flute, which dance, who Girdhari?
    The palace that you behold,
    Dazed, is actually his
    Whose crude jigs and jiggles
    Fetch diamond mines these days.

बहुत भोले हो सुदामा,
नहीं समझोगे इस कौतुक को...
मत भूलो अपने गाँवों को
जिनके विश्वासों की धूप-छाँह में कहीं
अभी भी बची है
एक जगमगाती द्वारिका
जिसमें रहता है कहीं
तुम्हारा वह पुराना सखा
जिसके साथ तुम
बचपन में खेला करते थे, और जो
केवल एक खिलौना नहीं।

You are simple, Sudama,
You won't understand this spectacle.
Do not forget your villages, your hamlets
In the sun and shadow of whose beliefs somewhere
A twinkling Dwarika
Still remains,
     Somewhere in which still lives
     That old friend of yours
     With whom you played in childhood
     And who was not
     Just a toy.

कुतुबमीनार

क्या हम अभी भी
उन्हीं नीचाइयों में खड़े हैं
जहाँ ऊँचाइयों का असर पड़ता है?

क्या ये सीढ़ियाँ हमें
उस सबसे ऊँची वाली जगह पर पहुँचा सकती हैं
जहाँ मीनारें ख़त्म हो जातीं
    और एक मस्तक शुरू होता
    ताजपोशी के लिए?

मेरे हाथों में एक दूरबीन है। मीनार
जिसके एक तरफ़ से मैं
    इतिहास के तमाम सितारों को देख रहा हूँ—
    उनके संसार जो अभी तक कहीं
    समय के चौथे आयाम में लक़दक़ हैं।

क्या मैं फिर किसी नये सितारे के समारोह में शामिल हूँ?
    या अँधेरी रातों में तारे गिन रहा हूँ?

Qutab Minar

Do we continue to stand
In those lowly grounds, where
Heights bedazzle to overpower us?

Do these stairways take us up
To that highest of high points
Where minars come to an end
        And a mind begins to be
        Honoured with the crown?

A spyglass in my hands. The minar
From one side of which I
        Behold the countless stars of history—
        Their constellations still aglitter somewhere
        In the fourth dimension of time. Am I

Again carousing in the pageant of some new superstar,
        Or counting stars in dark nights?

खजुराहो

गर्भगृह में आते ही एक आकस्मिक विचार—
कि मुझे विच्छिन्न करते हुए
उस प्रकाश से जो बाहर है
यदि बन्द हो जाए सदैव को प्रवेशद्वार
और मैं अकेला छूट जाऊँ
इन्हीं मूर्तियों के साथ
अपहृत इन्हीं के मायालोक में
इनके रूप पर आसक्त
खो जाऊँ मन्त्रमुग्ध प्यार की दैवी मुद्रा में
रह जाऊँ बन्दी इस समृद्ध सौन्दर्य का
कुछ इसी तरह जैसे ये
शार्दूल, अप्सराएँ, देवदासियाँ
शाल भंजिकाएँ,
कामलिप्त जोड़े
लजाती कुमारियाँ मुँह मोड़े

और तोरण के बाहर
एक दास की तरह प्रतीक्षा करता रह जाए
निस्पृह समय
किन्तु फिर कभी न खुले गर्भगृह।

और तभी लगा अकस्मात्
मूर्तियों के कोलाहल से भर उठा
मंडप, अन्तराल, अर्द्धमंडप

Khajuraho [17]

Entering the garbhagriha
in the womb of a temple
a sudden dream arose—what
if the ingress were to close
forever, untying me
from the light outside
and leaving me
all alone inside
    with these statues and glyphs,
    abducted into their dreamland
    enamoured of their allure
    entranced by postures of love, divinity
    …captive to this splendour of beauty,
    somewhat like these maidens
    apsaras devadasis shardools
    lion-bodied griffins and tree-nymphs
    couples entwined in desire
    virgins looking sideways

and outside the archways
stoical time
was left waiting like a slave,
    but the womb of the temple
    never opened again—

And then, suddenly it felt
a commotion of clattering statues filled up
mandapa, antaraala, ardhamandapa;

और उन सबने ज़िन्दा होकर
एक अश्लील प्रसव वेदना की शक्ति से
मुझे
तिलमिलाते प्रकाश में बाहर ढकेल दिया।

whereupon all of them came to life
and with the crude force
of a birth pang
      pushed me into the dazzle
         of the light outside

कुछ दिन अन्य देशकाल में

कुछ दिन अतिथि रहा
एक अन्य देशकाल की अनियत दिनचर्या में

बसा जैसे एक गाँव
स्मृतिविहीन
घटित हुआ जैसे एक फूल
इतिहास से परे
व्यतीत हुआ जैसे समय
बिना अतीत हुए

एक दिन
सुनता रहा घड़ी को रोककर
अपनी ही धड़कनों को
और जा निकला
किसी अन्तिम निष्कर्ष की तरह
एक ऐसे क्षितिज पर
जैसा एक बार सपने में देखा था

एक दिन
समुद्र के किनारे देखा
अपने सबसे महत्त्वकांक्षी मन को
दुर्दम लहरों की तरह उठते
और अपने ही सारांश में बिखर जाते

Some Days in Another Time, Another Place[18]

A visitor for some days
in the open timetable
of another time, another place

He settled like a village
without memory
happened like a flower
beyond history
passed like time
without becoming the past

One day
he stopped the clock and kept hearing
his own heartbeat,
then came out
like some final illation
on a horizon he once saw
in a dream

One day
he saw by the sea
his most zealous wish
billow out like frenetic waves
and scatter in his own depth

एक दिन हुआ
—जैसे सुबह
चला—जैसे हवा
बहा—जैसे नदी
सब जगह गया
लेकिन हर जगह बेपहचान
सबमें प्रवाहित हुआ
लेकिन अन्तर्ध्यान

एक दिन
प्रक्षिप्त एक विराट पर्दे पर
फैलकर देखा
अपनी सबसे विरल विद्यमानता को
अ-वस्तुगत होकर
एक अवाक् प्रार्थना में निवेदित होते

एक दिन
जिया एक शिलालेख
एक भित्ति-चित्र
एक पुराकथा—

अपने अनेक संस्करण, आलेख, पांडुलिपियाँ
खोजते हुए लाइब्रेरियों में, अजायबघरों में, विद्यालयों में
जा पहुँचा वहाँ
जहाँ केवल हर जानी जगह से—हर पायी वस्तु से—
लौट आना था एक ऐसे अविचल बिन्दु पर
जिसके चारों ओर
केवल एक अकुलाता विस्तार था
अपने लिए एक स्थिति खोजता हुआ

One day
he occurred—like a dawn
wandered—like a wind
meandered—like a river
went everywhere
but incognito
streamed into all
but invisible

One day
projected on a gigantic screen
he spread out and saw
his scarcest being
turn abstract
and become a speechless invocation

One day
he lived an epitaph
a fresco
a legend—

Searching his many editions, scripts, manuscripts
in libraries, museums and schools
he reached there
from where it was only a return—
from every known place, every acquired thing—
to a standstill,
unfaltering point... all around which
was just a fidgety expanse
seeking a situation for itself

एक दिन
पढ़ता रहा एक ऐसी विचित्र किताब
जिसमें भाषा के फन्दे न थे,
बड़े-से-बड़े विचारों की
शब्द बराबर छोटी-छोटी तस्वीरें थीं
बच्चों के खेलने लायक़...

अन्तिम दिन
भाषा और भाषा के अभेद से उत्पन्न वे
दिखे मुझे
जीवन की आत्मकथा
जो किसी भी देश किसी भी काल में
लिखी और पढ़ी जा सकती है,
जिसके लिए कहीं भी जन्म
कहीं भी मृत्यु सम्भव है,
जो किसी भी प्रस्तावना से पहले
या उपसंहार के बाद
    अनायास शुरू हो सकती है
      जैसे पुरुष
    किसी धरती पर प्रकट हो सकती है
      जैसे प्रकृति
    किसी आकाश में ध्वनित हो सकती है
      जैसे प्रेम

One day
he kept reading a strange book
that had no loops of language,
the biggest of ideas were tiny
word-sized images
with which children could play…

On the last day
he saw them, unaffected
by the difference between language and language—
life's saga of itself
that could be written and read
at any time in any land,
that could have been born
and could have died anywhere,
that preceding any prologue
or following any epilogue
    could all begin by itself
        like purusha
    could happen on any earth
        like prakriti
    could resound in any sky
        like love

The Wish of a Leaf

Sitting in a park
　　　I felt at peace

in the comfort of a tree's shade
　　　I felt at peace

a leaf fell from a twig,
the wish of a leaf
'now let us leave...'

contemplating this
　　　I felt at peace

आतिथ्य

कन्धों पर धूप की पीली चादर डाले
सड़क के किनारे चुपचाप खड़े
एक व्यक्ति-से लगते वृक्ष से मैंने पूछा
अतिथि-गृह का रास्ता...

वह चुप रहा,
फिर पूछा तब भी चुप रहा

मैं आगे बढ़ने को हुआ
तो लगा उसने कुछ कहा तो था...

शायद मैं ही उसकी भाषा को
नहीं समझ सका था, जो
     एक छाया की तरह विनम्र
     और एक मर्मर की तरह हार्दिक थी

Invitation

A yellow shawl of sunlight on its shoulders
standing quietly by the street
a tree that looked   like a person,
            I asked it the way to a rest house…

It remained silent,
I asked again, and still
            it remained silent

As I began to move ahead
            it felt   it did say something
                        after all

Maybe it was I, who had not understood
the language of one
                        that was
            gentle like a shade
            and intimate like a rustle

रामगढ़

शान्त स्थली

रूखेपन से बिलकुल अछूती
दूर-दूर तक फैली हरियाली
वह शान्त स्थली

मैंने उसे एक शब्दरहित
कविता सुनाई

वह सुनती रही चुपचाप
मंत्र-मुग्ध

राइटर्स होम

कमरे ख़ाली थे।
यहाँ ठहर सकता हूँ कुछ दिन—
    मैंने सोचा

तो उसके ख़ालीपन ने कहा—
    यहाँ 'कोई' या शायद 'कुछ'
    पहले ही से ठहरा है
    इतना अ-स्थानिक
    और इतना अव्यक्त
    कि उसके आरपार
    साफ़ दिखाई दे रही थी
    एक विश्राम की इच्छुक
    पहाड़-चढ़ती आकांक्षाओं की थकानें

नौकुचिया ताल

पहाड़ी जंगलों से लगभग ढँकी हुई
उस झील का निचाट अकेलापन
    कहने को नौ कोने
    पर एक भी कोना
    पूरी तरह उसका अपना नहीं।

मैं जाकर उसके अकेलेपन में
    अनायास शामिल हो गया
    और उसी की तरह अकेला हो गया

वह अकेलापन
आज भी मुझे
जब तब घेर लेता है

Ramgarh Triptych [19]

quiet space

untouched by aridity
a green grace
spread afar
that still space

i read to her
a wordless poem

she kept listening quietly
entranced

writer's home

empty rooms,
one could stay here
for a while—i thought

its emptiness spoke—
someone, something
stays here already,
so fleeting and so wordless
that one could clearly see
across it, the bleariness
of mountain-ascending longings
now keen to rest

naukuchiya taal

the unceasing loneliness
of that lake, mirror veiled
by mountains, woods,
nine corners to its name
but not even one
truly its own

i went and became one
with its loneliness, on my own,
and became alone like it...

even today, that loneliness
enwraps me now and then

अटूट हिस्सा

यह स्तब्धता सामान्य नहीं। असाधारण
कुछ होनेवाले से पहले की तैयारी है।
भीतर ही भीतर लुकेछिपे चलतीं गतिविधियाँ।

यह एक जंगल की चुप्पी नहीं।
तारों के झुरमुट में कोई है
हमें देख रहा। सुन रहा कोई
दिशाओं के कानों से। चल रही देर से
कोई गुपचुप कार्रवाई। दिये जा रहे गुप्त आदेश।

अचानक एक खलबली : पूरब की तरफ़
रोशनी की एक चीख़ के साथ
क्षितिज को फोड़ कर निकलता
ख़ून से सना एक शीश—दृष्य पर
एक विजय की आभा फेंकता हुआ।

इधर उधर भाग रहे
अँधेरे के मनहूस हत्यारे साये
फ़िलहाल छोड़कर मैदान
छिपने की जगहें खोजते हुए।

यह मनुष्यों के युद्धों और मारकाट के
इतिहासों से लिया गया
कोई छोटामोटा रक्तरंजित क़िस्सा नहीं :
पृथ्वी के जन्म से भी बहुत पहले से
चले आ रहे सृष्टि के तारान्तरीय जीवनक्रम का
अटूट हिस्सा है।

Unbroken

This stunned silence is not usual. It is
The harbinger of something momentous
About to happen. Within, hidden
Manoeuvres are going on unseen.

This is not the silence of a forest.
Someone out there is watching us
From a spinney of stars. Listening.
A wide sky is all ears. Some quiet deed
Will betide. Orders have been given secretly.

Suddenly, a commotion: from the east
A head bedraggled in blood
Comes bursting out of the horizon
With a scream of light—unfurling
An aureole of triumph across the vista.

Running helter-skelter, the ominous
Murderous shadows of darkness
Surrender the fray and field for now
Rummaging for places to hide.

This is not some trifling blood-sodden tale
Taken from human histories
Of wars and carnage:

Enduring on from long before the earth was
Born, it is a part of the interstellar
Life cycle of creation that remains
Unbroken.

नमदाफा के वर्षा-वन

अनवरत वर्षा में भीगती
वनस्पतियों से उठती
एक हरिहर ध्वनि—
  यह कोना अभी निर्माणाधीन है

नगाड़ों की तरह बजते बादल
उफनती नदियाँ
सागर तक ले जातीं
रसायनों के घोल
एक जटिल स्थापना
  अभी प्रयोगाधीन है

विभिन्न जीव-जन्तु
उनकी रूपरेखा का अटकल प्रारूप
एक जैविकी की सांकेतिका में निबद्ध
बंदर से आदमी तक की सूची
  अभी विचाराधीन है

आश्वस्त करता यह संयोग कि इस पृथ्वी की
परिचर्या में
अभी भी सुरक्षित हैं कुछ जगहें
  जो ईश्वर के अधीन हैं

The Rainforests of Namdapha

The viridescent echo of a numen
rises from the verdure
drenched in ceaseless rain
a corner still remains
    under creation

Clouds rumble like drums
frothing rivers heave
the soils and the elements
up to the sea's enigma
a hypothesis is still
    under experimentation

Contours of varied fauna
their conjectured atavistic modes
veiled in the codes of genes
from simian to man
a biotic index still
    under consideration

This coincidence reassures
that in nursing our earth
some dominions remain secure
—still quietly under
    celestial dispensation

पक्की सड़क के किनारे

बस यहीं तक एक पक्की सड़क है,
उसके आगे
सब कच्चा ही कच्चा

> एक कच्चा रास्ता,
> उसके दोनों ओर
> खर पतवार से ढकी
> एक कच्ची दीवार,
> फिर बहुत दूर तक
> एक पगडण्डी
> जो एक नाले को पार कर
> मेंड़ों से बँटे खेतों तक जाती,
> खेतों के पास
> एक कच्चे तालाब के किनारे
> एक घर...

कभी एक सपना देखा था
उस घर ने
कि एक पक्की सड़क
उस तक भी आयेगी,
प्यार से कहेगी—बाबा
लो हम आ गये
तुम्हारे बिल्कुल पास!

> खुशी से फूल उठेगा घर
> एक पुराने पेड़ की तरह
> पक्की सड़क के किनारे।

Next to a Paved Road

That's all, the tarmacked road
terminates here,
farther up
all is muddy all around

    a mud road,
    on either side of it
    a thatched wall of mud
    slathered with creepers and weeds,
    then a narrow, winding ribbon of a path
    that crosses over a runlet
    and zigzags far up into the fields
    parted by furrows and ridges of earth,
    touching the fields
    next to a muddy village pond
    a home…

That home
had dreamt sometime

that a paved road
would also come up to it
and lovingly say—grandpa,
look, we have come
so close to you, to live by your side now!

Then a home would bloom up with joy
    like an old tree
    next to a paved road.

जंगली गुलाब

वेर्नर हेर्ईज़ोग की फ़िल्म व्हेर द ग्रीन ऐंट्स ड्रीम को याद करते हुए

नहीं चाहिए मुझे
क़ीमती फूलदानों का जीवन

मुझे अपनी तरह
खिलने और मुरझाने दो
मुझे मेरे जंगल और वीराने दो

मत अलग करो मुझे
मेरे दरख़्त से
वह मेरा घर है
उसे मुझे अपनी तरह सजाने दो
उसके नीचे
पंखुड़ियों की शैय्या बिछाने दो

नहीं चाहिए मुझे किसी की दया
न किसी की निर्दयता
काट छाँट कर मुझे
सभ्य मत बनाओ

मुझे समझने की कोशिश मत करो
केवल सुरभि और रंगों से बना
मैं एक नाज़ुक ख़्वाब हूँ
            काँटों में पला
            जंगली गुलाब हूँ

Wild Rose

After Werner Herzog's *Where the Green Ants Dream*

no, we do not want
a life of opulent vases

let us
flower and wither
our own way, give us
our jungles our wilds

do not sever us
from our tree our home,
let us adorn it our way,
beneath it let us lay
our own pallet of petals

we want no charity
nor cruelty,
do not deracinate and clip us
or civilise us

do not try to unravel us,
created only
from colour and redolence
we are
        a fragile reverie
        weaned on thorns,
        wild roses

उदासी के रंग

उदासी भी
एक पक्का रंग है जीवन का

उदासी के भी तमाम रंग होते हैं
जैसे
फक्कड़ जोगिया
पतझरी भूरा
फीका मटमैला
आसमानी नीला
वीरान हरा
बर्फ़ीला सफेद
बुझता लाल
बीमार पीला

कभी-कभी धोखा होता
उल्लास के इंद्रधनुषी रंगों से खेलते वक़्त
कि कहीं वे
किन्हीं उदासियों से ही
छीने हुए रंग तो नहीं?

Colours of Melancholy

Melancholy too
is a lasting colour of life

with many a tint and hue

    vagrant ochre
    yonder blue
    autumnal fallow
    jaundiced yellow
    deserted green
    pallid russet
    frost cold white
    snuffed out red

Every now and then, one is tricked
when cavorting with the rainbow colours of joy

—were they perhaps not

colours stolen
from some melancholies, too?

सुनयना

कई बार ऐसा हुआ
कि वैसा नहीं हुआ
जैसा होना चाहिए था...

कैसा होना चाहिए था
फूल-सी सुनयना की आँखों में
अपने प्रेम में विश्वास का रंग?

वैसा नहीं मिला मौसम
जिसमें खिलते हैं फूल
अपनी समस्तता में
निश्छल और चंचल एक साथ।

                    *

कुछ लोग उसे देखने आये
देखने की तारीख़ से पहले,
ख़रीद की तर्ज़ पर पक्की कर गये उसे
पकने की तारीख़ से पहले।

तूफ़ानों से लड़ती
एक अकेली पत्ती
दरख़्त की उँगली पकड़े...

उसके विश्वास का रंग
अब वैसा था जैसा होता है
डाल से तोड़े हुए फूलों का रंग।

                    *

Sunayana [20]

It often happened
that it did not happen
the way it should have been...

How should have been
in flower-like Sunayana's eyes
the colour of faith in her love?

The seasons came her way
not the full way
in which flowers bloom,
guileless and sparkling.

*

Some people came to her
without her wanting,
a season came to pass
before she could say a thing.

Taking on tempests
a lone leaf clutching
a tree's finger...

The colour of her faith
was now what is
the colour of blossoms after plucking.

*

...पिछली बार अयोध्या में
कनकभवन की सीढ़ियों से उतरते देखा उसे—
भस्म अंगों में वैसा न था यौवन
जैसा होना चाहिए था
ऐसे भरे फागुन में टेसू का रंग!

अब वह
सूर्यास्त समय
जैसे नदी पार के घिरते अँधेरे में
घुलता चला जाय एक बजरे का रंग
ऐसा था ऐसे समय
हाथों में फूल लिये
उसका चुपचाप कहीं
ओझल हो जाने का ढंग।

...Last time in Ayodhya
she was seen descending
the Kanakbhavan steps—
in her ashen limbs was not the vim
as there should have been
the flush of tesu in such a full spring.

Now she
in sundown time
like the fading blur of a barge,
a hue that goes on dissolving,
on the other side of the river, in the setting dark—
such was in this time
quietly somewhere, flowers in hand,
the manner of her disappearing.

गौरैया

पिता के अन्तिम दिनों में
उनसे बहुत हिल-मिल गई थी एक गौरैया,
कभी-कभी पास आकर बैठ जाती
और देर तक निहारती रहती उन्हें...

पिता कहते थे उसकी भोली आँखों से झाँकती है
एक माँ की वत्सल आत्मा।

गाती है चिड़िया
दूर कहीं वृक्षों के झुरमुट में
सुनाती है शायद अपने बच्चों को
अपनी भाषा में अपना कोई अटपटा गीत
जो गूँजता है दुनिया भर की भाषाओं में
अलग अलग तरह

चाहता हूँ वह उड़कर मेरे पास आए
मुझसे सटकर बैठ जाए
और सुनाए मुझे पहले
अपने कुछ गीत,
फिर गाए मेरे उन गीतों को
जिन्हें शायद अब मैं कभी न लिख पाऊँगा।

पोंछे अपने कोमल पंखों से मेरे आँसुओं को,
उठा उठा कर मेरा खाना थाली से
मुझे दाना दाना चुगाए

A Sparrow's Song

A sparrow grew fond of father
in his last days, it would come
and sit beside him
beholding him for hours;

Father used to say, from its eyes
gazed a mother's doting soul.

A bird chirrups a song somewhere
far in a cluster of trees, perhaps
sings to its fledglings
some quaint little song
in a tongue of its own
that all the world's languages echo
in motley ways

I want it to fly and come to me,
sit close to me, sing to me
its own songs first,
then those songs of mine
I may never be able to write now…

Let it wipe my tears with its tender wings,
pick from my plate crumb by crumb
and feed me morsel by morsel,

मेरे परेशान माथे को
सहलाकर मुझे सुलाए
और सपनों में भी मुझसे कभी दूर न हो

और उस दिन जब वह उड़े तो
मेरे प्राणों को भी अपने साथ लेकर
दूर कहीं उड़ जाए...

coddle my anxious brow,
lull me gently to sleep, and even
in my dreams never leave me;

And when it flies off that day,
let it take me along
and fly somewhere far away.

जंगल की किताब

किताब बहुत पुरानी थी
और जंगल उससे भी ज़्यादा पुराना।

लगभग हर पंक्ति के नीचे पेंसिल के गहरे निशान थे,
मुझसे पहले जिसने भी पढ़ा था उसे
बहुत मेहनत से पढ़ा था।

कुछ देर बाद मुझे लगा मैं पढ़ नहीं रहा
पेंसिल के निशानों पर चल रहा हूँ
जो पगडण्डियों में बदल गए थे,
उनके दोनों तरफ़ शब्दों के घने जंगल थे।
हर शब्द एक अलग जाति के वृक्ष की तरह था
जिनसे मिलकर बनता था भाषा का महावन।

कई बार पगडण्डियों से ऊब कर सोचा—
उन्हें छोड़ कर जंगल में प्रवेश करूँ
जो इतना दुर्गम और रहस्यमय दीखता था।
पर सीधी रेखा को पकड़ कर चलने के पाँव
इतने अभ्यस्त हो चुके थे
कि दरख़्तों के बीच बिना पंख उड़ने की कल्पना भी
असंगत लगती थी।

अचानक मैंने असाधारण थकान महसूस की।
राहें और जंगल अभी भी
उतने ही निगूढ़ और अपार लग रहे थे।

The Book of the Forest

Kilbury Forest, Kumaon

The book was old
and the forest even older.

Almost under every line were deep pencil marks,
Whoever read it before me
must have read it diligently.

After a time it felt like I
wasn't reading but walking
on the pencil marks that had transformed
into trails, with dense jungles of words
on both sides. Each word a tree
of a distinct species, which together formed
the grand greenwood of language.

Bored of trails, I often
thought—let us leave them
and straggle into the jungle that looked
impossible and mysterious.
But my feet had got so used
to walking along a straight line
that even to imagine flying without wings
amidst coverts and trees
seemed discordant.

Then, I felt an unusual tiredness.
Paths and jungles still appeared
inexhaustible and obscure as before.

मैं कहीं कुछ देर
बैठकर विश्राम करना चाहता था।

मैंने अपने आसपास घूमकर देखा—
आश्चर्य,
वहाँ केवल जंगल और राहें थीं...

बीच में न कहीं विराम न अर्ध-विराम

किताब के अन्त में
केवल एक पूर्ण-विराम।

192

I wanted to sit down and rest
for a while somewhere

I looked around me and saw—
amazement!
only jungles and paths were there...

in the middle nowhere
no caesura no stop
nor even a colon or half-stop

only a full-stop
at the end of the book.

पानी की प्यास

धरती में प्रवेश करती
पानी की प्यास
    पाना चाहती जिस गहराई को
    वह पहुँच से दूर थी,

कई तहों को पार करती
एक पारदर्शी तरलता को
    मिट्टी के रन्ध्र
    धीरे-धीरे सोख रहे थे।

देवदार की जड़ों से
अभी और बहुत नीचे तक जाना था पानी को
    कि सहसा खिंचकर
    उसकी जड़ों में समा गया वह
    और तेज़ी से ऊपर उठने लगा।

जिस शिखर तक पहुँचा
वह बेशक़ बादलों को छू रहा था,
    पर था वह अब भी
    एक वृक्ष का ही शरीर—
    वही मरमर
    वही हवा में साँस लेने का स्वर
    चिड़ियों का घर
    वही बसन्त, वही वर्षा, वही पतझर।

The Thirst of Water

Entering the earth,
the thirst of water wished
to reach a depth
far away from reach

Navigating manifold tiers,
a transparent fluidity
was slowly being soaked
into the porous soil

From the roots of the cedar
the water had to go deeper
    when it was suddenly drawn
    into the roots of the tree
    and started rising up rapidly.

The pinnacle it reached
undoubtedly touched the nimbus,
    but it was still
    very much the body of a tree—
    the same rustle
    same rhythm of breathing in the air
    the birds' bustle
    same spring, rain, leaf-fall, everywhere—

वहाँ से फिर ऊपर उठकर
आकाश हो जाने की सम्भावना
अभी ओझल थी।

नहीं, उसने सोचा, फिर नहीं लौटना है उसे
धूल में
झरते फूल पत्तों के संग

उसने एक लम्बी साँस ली हवा में
और बादलों के साथ हो लिया।

अद्भुत था पृथ्वी का दृश्य
उस ऊँचाई से
अपनी ओर खींचता
उसका प्रबल आकर्षण
उसकी सोंधी उसांस :

वही था इस रोमांस का
सबसे नाजुक क्षण
उत्कर्ष के चरम बिन्दु पर थरथराती
एक बूँद की अदम्य अभिलाषा
कि लुढ़क कर बादलों से
चूम ले अपनी मिट्टी को फिर एक बार
भरकर अपने प्रगाढ़ आलिंगन में

The possibility of rising again from there
and becoming the empyreal blue
was still a haze.

No, it thought, it mustn't
return to dust again
with the falling leaves and flowers

It took a deep breath in the air
and became one with the clouds…

The vista of the earth was resplendent
from those heights
        drawing towards itself
        its magnetic attraction
        its earthy sigh its petrichor:

That was the most delicate and oracular
moment of this romance
        quivering at the ultimate zenith of ascent

        the quenchless yearning of a droplet
                that it tumble down from the firmament
                and kiss its earth once more,
                taking it back in its embrace.

The Myriad
Languages of Love

There was so much in the world
to fight and vie for
to kill and die for

But the heart I got was such
that it stayed lost in a bit of love
and life went on...

मारिषा

इतनी अनांगिक सुंदरता
कि एक काया में न समाती

बार बार लौटती है
विभिन्न शरीरों में
विभिन्न देशों और समयों में

कभी हेलेन, कभी क्लिओपैट्रा,
    कभी कारमेन...

कहती वह—मेरा पीछा मत करना,
    प्रतीक्षा करना
मैं स्वयं ही आऊँगी तुम्हारे जीवन में,

मैं भोर की बहती हवाओं की तरह
अस्थिर हूँ
    फूलों पर चमकते
ओस-कणों की तरह क्षणिक
    स्पर्श से परे एक कवि का स्वप्न

मुझे पहली बार ऋषियों ने
एक ऋग्वन में देखा था
इतनी आत्मिक
कि एक देह तक नहीं

Marisha[21]

such a bodiless beauty
that one form couldn't contain it

she returns again and again
to different bodies
in disparate places, distinct times

sometimes helen sometimes cleopatra
        sometimes carmen...

do not chase me, says marisha,
        wait for me
i will come to your life on my own

desultory
        like the fleeting winds of dawn
momentary
        like gleaming dewdrops on flowers
i am a poet's dream beyond touch;

sages saw me for the first time
in a rigvedic forest,
so soulful so seraphic
that there wasn't even
        any body
                at all

उजास

तब तक इजिप्ट के पिरामिड नहीं बने थे
जब दुनिया में
    पहले प्यार का जन्म हुआ

तब तक आत्मा की खोज भी नहीं हुई थी,
    शरीर ही सब कुछ था

काफ़ी बाद विचारों का जन्म हुआ
    मनुष्य के मस्तिष्क से

अनुभवों से उत्पन्न हुईं स्मृतियाँ
    और जन्म-जन्मांतर तक
      खिंचती चली गईं

माना गया कि आत्मा का वैभव
    वह जीवन है जो कभी नहीं मरता

प्यार ने
शरीर में छिपी इसी आत्मा के
    उजास को जीना चाहा।

एक आदिम देह में
    लौटती रहती है वह अमर इच्छा
रोज़ अँधेरा होते ही
      डूब जाती है वह
        अँधेरे के प्रलय में

First Light

The pyramids of Egypt had not been built
when the first love was
    born in the world

The search for a soul, too,
had not begun
    till then, the body was everything.

Thoughts took birth much later
from the mind, memories were born
    from experience… and stretched on
    for life after life

It came to be believed
that the soul's splendour
    was the life that never dies;

Love—wished to live
    the dawn of this undying soul
    mantled in body and flesh.

That wish of eternity
keeps returning again and again
inside a primeval body;

Daily as dusk descends
    it drowns down
        in a deluge of darkness

और हर सुबह निकलती है
एक ताज़ी वैदिक भोर की तरह
पार करती है
सदियों के अंतराल और अपाट दूरियाँ
अपने उस अर्धांग तक पहुँचने के लिए
जिसके बार बार लौटने की कथाएँ
एक देह से लिपटी हैं।

and rises again each morning
like a new vedic dawn,
    traverses
    a hiatus of centuries and fathomless distances
    to reach its other half

the tales of whose eternal returns
    stay embraced to a body.

अद्यापि...

संदर्भ : चौर-पंचाशिका

आज भी
कदली के गहन झुरमुटों में
एक संकेत की प्रतीक्षा करता हुआ कवि
देखता है किसी अँधेरी शताब्दी में
तुम्हारा सौन्दर्य
एक दीये-सा जगमगाता है।

आज भी
तुम्हारे कौमार्य का कंचन-वैभव
कड़े पहरों में
एक राजमहल की तरह
दूर से झिलमिलाता है।

आज भी
तुम्हारे यौवन के एक गुलाबी मौसम से उड़ कर
बेचैन कर जानेवाली हवाओं का
लड़खड़ाता झोंका
फूलों के रंगीन गवाक्षों से आता है।

आज भी
हमारी ढीठ वासनाओं के चोर-दरवाज़ों से होता हुआ
एक सँकरा रास्ता
लुकता छिपता
तुम्हारे शयनकक्ष तक जाता है।

Chaur Panchashika: Even Today…

Even today, in the thickets
of a banana grove,
a poet waits for a clue
and beholds in some dark century
your beauty shimmer like a lamp.

Even today, the aureate
cornucopia of your maidenhood
under stringent vigil
like a regal palace
glimmers from far away.

Even today, a gust of wind
that leaves one restless
rises from a rose-tinted season of your spring
and emerges teetering
from the iridescent skylights of flowers.

Even today, passing through
the clandestine doors of our bold passions
like a thief, a narrow passage
lurking and hiding
reaches the recesses of your chamber.

आज भी
नंगी पीठ से चिपकी तुम्हारी कामातुर हथेलियाँ
तुम्हारे बेसब्र समर्पण को स्वीकारता पौरुष
तुम्हें एक छन्द की तरह रचता
और एक उत्सव की तरह मनाता है।

आज भी
तुम एक गीत हो सूनी घाटियों में गूँजता हुआ
जो रात के तीसरे पहर
अपने पंखुरी-से ओठों को कानों पर रख कर
धीरे से जगाता है।

आज भी
किसी प्राचीन अनुशासन की ऊँची अटारी पर कैद
राजकन्या-सा प्यार
एक सामान्य कवि को
स्वीकार करने का साहस दिखाता है।

आज भी
उसकी आँखें तुम्हें एक नींद की तरह सोतीं—
एक स्वप्न की तरह देखतीं—
एक याद की तरह जीती हुई रातों का
वह अन्तराल है
जो कभी नहीं भर पाता है।

आज भी
तुम्हारे साथ जी गई पचास रातों का एक वसंत
प्रतिवर्ष जीवन का कोना कोना
अपनी सम्पूर्ण कलाओं से भर जाता है।

Even today, your desirous
palms press against his naked back,
a manhood receives your impatient abandon,
begets you like a verse
and celebrates you like a fête.

Even today, you are a song
echoing in lonesome valleys
that in the third quarter of the night
puts its petal-lips on his ears
and wakes him up gently.

Even today, held captive
in the high attic of some ancient order,
the love of a royal princess
dares to embosom
an ordinary poet.

Even today, his eyes
sleep you like a slumber,
see you like a dream—
that interlude of nights, alive
like a remembrance, never fills.

Even today, a springtide
of fifty nights lived with you
imbues with all its love-acts
every little corner of life
each year.

आज भी
एक कवि काल को सम्मुख रख
कठोरतम राजाज्ञा की अन्तिम अवज्ञा में
'विद्या' और 'सुन्दर' की वर्जित प्रेमलीलाओं को
शब्दों की मनमानी ऋतुओं से सजाता है।

आज भी
एक दरबार का पराजित अहं
क्षमा का ढोंग रचता
और विजयी प्यार के सामने
अपना सिर झुकाता है।

Even today, a poet confronts
his destined time—in final
disregard of a despotic decree—
and adorns with the wanton seasons of words
the forbidden love-sagas of Vidya and Sundar.

Even today, the defeated
ego of a kingly court
feigns to forgive—
then bows its head down
to the triumph of love.

प्यार की भाषाएँ

मैंने कई भाषाओं में प्यार किया है

पहला प्यार
    ममत्व की तुतलाती मातृभाषा में—
    कुछ ही वर्ष रही वह जीवन में

दूसरा प्यार
    बहन की कोमल छाया में
    एक सेनेटोरियम की उदासी तक

फिर नासमझी की भाषा में
एक लौ को पकड़ने की कोशिश में
    जला बैठा था अपनी उँगलियाँ

एक पर्दे के दूसरी तरफ़
खिली धूप में खिलता गुलाब
बेचैन शब्द
    जिन्हें ओठों पर लाना भी गुनाह था

धीरे-धीरे जाना
प्यार की और भी भाषाएँ हैं दुनिया में
    देशी-विदेशी

और विश्वास किया कि प्यार की भाषा
    सब जगह एक ही है
लेकिन जल्दी ही जाना
    कि वर्जनाओं की भाषा भी एक ही है :

The Languages of Love

I have loved in myriad languages...

The first time
in the lisping mother-tongue of filial love
    —her sojourn in life was short, evanescent

The second time
in sister's tender shadow
    down to the lingering sorrow of a sanatorium

Then, in a language of brazenness
I had singed my fingers
    trying to touch a flame

On the other side of a screen
a rose blooms in the rapturous sun, restless words
    that mustn't be brought to the lips

Little by little, I learnt that love
had a sea of voices in the world
    —familiar, foreign—

And believed that love far and wide
had the same dialects, but trammels to it
    had the same sociolects, idiolects too

एक-से घरों में रहते हैं
तरह-तरह के लोग
　　जिनसे बनते हैं
　　दूरियों के भूगोल...

अगला प्यार
भूली बिसरी यादों की
ऐसी भाषा में जिसमें शब्द नहीं होते
　　केवल कुछ अधमिटे अक्षर
　　कुछ अस्फुट ध्वनियाँ भर बचती हैं
　　जिन्हें किसी तरह जोड़कर
　　हम बनाते हैं
　　　　प्यार की भाषा

प्यार की भाषाएँ

मैंने अनेक भाषाओं में प्यार किया है

पहला प्यार
ममत्व की तुतलाती भाषाभाषा में...
　　कुछ ही वर्ष कलिका रही वह जीइसे है :

दूसरा प्यार
बहन की सिक्त [छाया] में　　कोमल
　　एक सेंटेटेरिज्म की उदासी तक :

फिर नारायणन की भाषा में
　（गे）　एक हँसी को पकड़ने की कोशिश में
　　बना बैठा घर अपनी दीवारें　（दूरी）
　　एक धूप के दूसे तरफ
（नेमीज）　किसी धूप में खिलता गुलाब
　　जिन्हें कोठों पर लाना भी गुनाह था :

धीरे-धीरे जाना
प्यार की और भी भाषाएँ हैं दुनिया में
　　देरी [बिदेशी]
लेकिन इतनी ही जाना
　　कि बचनाओं की भाषा भी एक ही है :

एक-से घरों में रहते हैं
तरह[तरह के लोग
　　जिनसे बनते हैं
　　दूरियों के भूगोल..

अगला प्यार
भूली बिसरी यादों की
ऐसी भाषा में जिसमें शब्द नहीं होते
　　केवल कुछ [अधमिटे]　अक्षर
　　कुछ अस्फुट ध्वनियां भर बचती है
　　जिन्हें किसी भी तरह जोड़ कर
　　हम बनाते हैं आती प्यार की भाषा

214

In the same sorts of houses
live disparate sorts of people, and thus are begotten
    the geographies of distances…

The next love, now,
in a drifting idiom of old
    half-forgotten remembrances

in which there are no words
only some half-erased alphabets
    some blurred echoes that still linger

    which we, somehow, piece together
    and again create a new
        language of love…

निसर्ग

मुझे पसन्द है उसकी देह का सरल भूरापन
उसके शरीर की माटी–पानी–गन्ध
धीमे बहती हवा की तरह उसका पास से गुज़रना
धूप की तरह खिलखिलाना

    रात वह केवल एक आभास है
    किसी गहरी घाटी में बहते प्रवाह का—
    कभी चाँदनी की तरह कोमल
    कभी आँधी की तरह बेसब्र

जूड़ा खोल कर सोयी थी रात जो बाँहों में
उसके अभिप्रायों को जता कर
हँस देता है पवन

मैंने एक बार उसकी आँखों से
उसके अन्दर झाँक कर देखा है
उसकी वासनाओं के गुप्त अतल में...
    एक नदी बहती
    आदिम जंगलों से लगभग ढकी हुई घाटी में
    एक स्वप्न तैर आता कुहरे-सा
    उस नदी के ऊपर ऊपर

तल्लीन उँगलियाँ
मछलियों की तरह खेलतीं
अँधेरी गहराइयों से छूटते जल में

और एक विश्राम
उठ आता कभी कभी
शान्ति की हद तक...

Being Nature

I like the easy brown of her body,
the earth-water-smell of her flesh,
her gliding by, gently like the wafting air
giggling like sunlight

> The night, she's only a semblance
> of a stream that drifts, in some deep vale—
> sometimes tender like moonlight
> sometimes restive like a storm

She who slept the night in embrace
with her hair all undone—
the wind reveals her intent,
laughing with abandon

Through her eyes, I have once
peeped inside of her and seen
into the orphic abyss of her desires...
a river flows

> in a glen nearly mantled
> with primeval forests
> a dream floats up like a fog
> frothing up above that river

Rapt fingers frolic about
like fish in water
that the dark depths release...

And a calm repose
that sometimes extends
all the way to   peace...

बारिश में भीगने से पहले

वह मुझे
मेरी किसी कविता में नहीं
अपनी कहानी में मिली—

वह भी शुरू में नहीं,
एक औसत पारिवारिक कहानी के
बीच में कहीं, अकस्मात्...

तब तक आधी से ज़्यादा
उसकी सुंदरता ख़त्म हो चुकी थी
और उसका अधेड़ जीवन
ज़मीन जायदाद की तरह पंजीकृत हो चुका था
उसके पति और बच्चों के नाम।

हम दोनों हाथ में हाथ डाले
एक घुमावदार पहाड़ी ढलान से
नीचे उतर रहे थे

बरसने को उतावले घने काले बादलों से
ढक गयी थीं—शिखर से आकाश तक—
उड़ान की हदें

बारिश में भीगने से पहले
उसे घर लौटने की जल्दी थी।

Before Getting Drenched
in the Rain

I met her
not in a poem of mine
but in a story

and not in the beginning either,
but somewhere in the middle
of an ordinary homely story, suddenly...

By then half her beauty had ebbed
and the remainder of her life
had been registered like land
in the name of her family.

The two of us, hand in hand,
were descending down
a craggy, roundabout mountain slope

From summit to sky
dense caliginous clouds impatient to rain
had hemmed in the limits of flight.

Before getting drenched in the rain
she was in a hurry to return home.

तेलीमेना

पोलिश कवि मीच्क्येविच के पान तादेउष पर

इस में हर्ज ही क्या था
अगर प्रौढ़ा नायिका ने दोनों को चाहा एक साथ?

युवक को उसकी जवानी के लिए
और वयस्क को उसकी अक्लमंदी के लिए

अगर दोनों को एक ही में पाना मुश्किल था
तो दोनों को अलग अलग चाहना
आख़िर ग़लत क्यों था?

तुम भले ही हँसो मीच्क्येविच...

लेकिन सच तो यह है
कि दया की पात्र नहीं—
यौवन और बुद्धि के संयोग की
अद्भुत उदाहरण थी तेलीमेना

Telimena

On Mickiewicz's *Pan Tadeusz*

What was wrong with it after all
if the mature lady desired
both at once?

> The young man for his youth,
> the adult for his nous

If she couldn't get both in one
why was it so wrong after all
to separately covet both?

You may well snigger, Mickiewicz...

But the truth surely is
she wasn't an object of pity—
> an extraordinary instance
> of the wise and the vernal
> in unison, herself
> was Telimena

नई किताबें

नई नई किताबें पहले तो
दूर से देखती हैं मुझे
　　शरमाती हुई

फिर संकोच छोड़ कर
बैठ जाती हैं फैल कर
　　मेरे सामने मेरी पढ़ने की मेज़ पर

उनसे पहला परिचय... स्पर्श
हाथ मिलाने जैसी रोमांचक
　　एक शुरुआत

धीरे धीरे खुलती हैं वे
पृष्ठ दर पृष्ठ
घनिष्ठतर निकटता
　　कुछ से मिलता
　　कुछ से गहरी मिलता
　　कुछ अनायास ही छू लेतीं मेरे मन को
　　कुछ मेरे चिंतन का अंग बन जातीं
　　कुछ पूरे परिवार की पसंद
ज़्यादातर ऐसी जिनसे कुछ न कुछ मिल जाता

फिर भी
अपने लिए हमेशा खोजता रहता हूँ
किताबों की इतनी बड़ी दुनिया में
　　एक जीवन-संगिनी

New-Found Books

They look at me
from a distance first
    coyly

Then unabashedly
stretch out and sit
    on my desk before me

The first acquaintance with them... the first touch
thrilling like a handshake
    a new beginning

Page by page then, they open up slowly,
a greater intimacy
    —friendship with some,
    with some a deeper affection,
    some touch my heart
    become my thoughts,
    some part of the family—
most mean something to me

Even so
in this vast world of books
I go on searching
    for a life-companion
    for myself,

थोड़ी अल्हड़-चुलबुली-सुंदर
आत्मीय किताब

जिसके सामने मैं भी खुल सकूँ
एक किताब की तरह पन्ना पन्ना
और वह मुझे भी
प्यार से मन लगा कर पढ़े

a carefree, blithe, lively
book of my own

before whom I too could open up
leaf and page, like a book

and she would also then read me
with rapt attention, lovingly

कविता

कविता वक्तव्य नहीं गवाह है
कभी हमारे सामने
कभी हमसे पहले
कभी हमारे बाद

कोई चाहे भी तो रोक नहीं सकता
भाषा में उसका बयान
जिसका पूरा मतलब है सचाई
जिसकी पूरी कोशिश है बेहतर इन्सान

उसे कोई हड़बड़ी नहीं
कि वह इश्तहारों की तरह चिपके
जुलूसों की तरह निकले
नारों की तरह लगे
और चुनावों की तरह जीते

वह आदमी की भाषा में
कहीं किसी तरह ज़िन्दा रहे, बस

Poetry

1

it is not a declaration, but a witness
sometimes before us
sometimes after us
sometimes ahead of us

even if one wants one cannot stop
its testimony in language
which only means truth,
only seeks a gentler being

it is in no scramble
to be pasted up like ads
marched out like parades
chanted like slogans
or won like elections

in the language of people, it be
alive somewhere, somehow, that's all

कविता की ज़रूरत

बहुत कुछ दे सकती है कविता
क्यों कि बहुत कुछ हो सकती है कविता
    ज़िन्दगी में
         अगर हम जगह दें उसे
जैसे फूलों को जगह देते हैं पेड़
जैसे तारों को जगह देती है रात

हम बचाये रख सकते हैं उसके लिए
अपने अन्दर कहीं
    ऐसा एक कोना
जहाँ ज़मीन और आसमान
जहाँ आदमी और भगवान के बीच दूरी
    कम से कम हो...

वैसे कोई चाहे तो जी सकता है
    एक नितान्त कवितारहित ज़िन्दगी
      कर सकता है
        कवितारहित प्रेम

2

it can give a lot
for so much can be poetry
    in life, if we give it space
as trees give space to flowers
as nights give space to stars

we can keep saved for it
somewhere inside of us, a corner
where the schism between earth and sky
between people and God
    is the least...

of course, if one wants
one can
    love without poetry
    live without poetry

शाम की सैर

सूरज के डूबने
और अँधेरा होने के बीच
अभी भी बचा है
एक सैर का वक़्त

आसपास इतना सुदूर
जैसे क्षितिज
न पास लगता पास
न दूर   दूर
        यानी कि दिन डूबे   इससे पहले
        पहले तारे के निकलने का वक़्त

आओ, कुछ दूर तक चलें साथ हम तुम
जब तक बचा है हमारे पास
        एक बेसिर-पैर की हवाख़ोरी का वक़्त

घिरते अँधेरे में
उस पेड़ के नीचे
        आँखें मीचे
        दो लिपटी परछाइयाँ
              अलविदा से पहले
              गले मिलने का वक़्त

A Twilight Stroll

between sunset
and darkness, there
is still some time
for a little stroll

the nearnesses so faraway
like the horizon
the near doesn't look near
nor the far   that far
        before the day   can disappear
        time for the first star to appear

come, let us wend our way together
some distance further, you and I,
        till there is still left with us
        time for a bootless saunter

in the enfolding darkness
under that tree there
        eyes shut
        two shadows clinging
                before the farewell
                time to embrace

निकटता

अकेलापन एक तरह की दूरी है
    अपने से

कभी-कभी कहीं दूर
छोड़ कर अपने को
लौट आता हूँ परायों के पास,
पराये की तरह सोचता हूँ—
    यह कैसा आसपास
    जिसमें सभी दूर दूर।

अनायास एक दूरी से कहता—'हेलो, दूरी!'
वह हँस देती।

हँसी भी एक तरह की निकटता है।

एक ढीठ उत्प्रेक्षा
    मेरे पास सरक आती

न जाने कितनी दूरियों को दूर ढकेलते हुए।

Nearness

Loneliness is a kind of separation
    from one's own   self

Sometimes I leave myself
somewhere far away
and come back, amidst strangers,
I think like a stranger—
    what proximities are these
    where all are a distance away.

Suddenly, I say to a distance—
'Hello, distance.' And she laughs.

Laughter is also a kind of nearness.

An emboldened fancy
moves up close to me

    pushing so many distances aside.

मेरे इतने पास

समय बहुत कम है फिर भी
कुछ दिनों जी कर तुम्हारे साथ
जीवन-प्रसंग में जोड़ना चाहता हूँ
एक उप-संसार

जैसे अचानक याद आ जाए
एक अनुभव पुनश्च :

गर्मी के दिनों में
पहाड़ों की सैर
रिमझिम वर्षा में
किसी भूली-बिसरी झील के किनारे
किसी अज्ञात डाक-बंगले में
बिताना चाहता हूँ
एक समाप्तक युग की बाक़ी छुट्टियाँ।
कस्तूरी-सी उठती देह-गन्ध से नहाना चाहता हूँ,
जीना चाहता हूँ पूरी आसक्ति से
इतना मादक कुछ
जो जीवन में पहले-पहले प्यार से भी
कहीं अधिक रोमांचक हो...

अरे, यह ज़रा-सी धूप
कमरे से बाहर जाते जाते
अचानक क्यों
मेरे इतने पास सरक आई है?

Postscript: So Close to Me

The Lower Himalayas

Time is short, and still
I wish to live with you
for a few days
and thus attach a sub-world
to this narrative of life

Like a rare interlude
suddenly remembered, postscript:

In the August days
a sojourn to the hills,
in the hushed pitter-patter of rain
by a half-forgotten lake
in some nameless retreat,
I wish to beguile
the remaining days of this ending epoch;
to bathe in your musky fragrance
to live in complete captivation
of something intoxicating
and even more exhilarating
than the first love in life...

Oh, why has this tiny patch of sunlight
that was about to leave the room
now suddenly moved
so close to me?

Pass, Something
Pass Us By

Why does it seem all the time
all around me are only eyes
that are able to see only me
not the wonder that I see

nor even that pain of all
which I live all the time
nor even the cosmic carnival of creation
made of an unbearable loneliness

शब्द तक

व्यर्थ है
बहुत दूर तक उसे सोचना
जो आसमान में एक बिन्दु भर जगह
और पल भर समय में संचित है।

मैं तब की बात कर रहा हूँ
जब तुम रुकोगे कुछ देर

अभी बहुत उतावली में हो
कहीं और जाने की
कुछ और पाने की
कुछ से कुछ और हो जाने की...

बात तब की है
जब केवल मेरे शब्द होंगे मेरी जगह

तब उस विकलता को समझोगे
जो सब कुछ—शब्द तक—
यहीं छोड़ जाने में होती है।

Words Too Are Left Behind

It is futile
to think very far of that
which is contained within
a minim in the sky
and a moment in time.

I am talking of then
when you will slow down for a bit

You are in a great hurry right now
      to go somewhere else
      to get something else
      to grow into someone else...

I am speaking of then
when only my words will remain
instead of me.

Then you will understand the unease
      that is there in leaving
behind everything here
            —even words.

शव-परीक्षा

सन्दर्भ: अमरपक्षी फ़ीनिक्स का मिथक

मानो किसी अमूर्त को मूर्त करता वह एक अक्षर मंत्र था।
कुछ था जो बेचैन करता था
उन आँखों की बिल्लौरी चमक में,
किसी गूढ़ार्थ की तड़ित-कौंधें
उसकी उड़ानों के बेढंगे यमक में।
लोगों की घबराहटों में उसकी हत्या का पूरा षड्यंत्र था।

एक दिन, किसी के हाथों जब वह मार कर लाया गया,
सब दंग थे कि उसके पंख उससे
किताब के पन्नों की तरह जुड़े थे,
वे अब भी फड़फड़ा रहे थे हवा में
जो कभी एक असीम में उड़े थे।
वह शून्य से भी अधिक हल्का लगा जब उसे उठाया गया।

कितनी अजीब थी अब उस सौन्दर्य के मरण की प्रतीक्षा
जो असंख्य हत्याओं बाद भी
न तो मरता न हाथ आता,
उसे जला कर जो राख कर डालती
फिर उसी आग के डैने बनाता।
व्यर्थ थी अमरत्व की खोज में अब उसकी शव-परीक्षा।

240

Post-Mortem of a Phoenix

Giving form to the formless, as if it were a magic rune—
something was disquieting there
in its eyes and their crystal light,
lightning flashes of some insight
in the gauche echo of its flight.
In the nescience of people, lay the plot to kill it soon.

When it was slain by someone, and brought in one day,
all were dazed its wings stuck to it
like pages to a book's body,
they still fluttered in the wind—
which once soared in eternity.
It seemed lighter than the void, when lifted away.

How eerie was this wait now, for the dying of that beauty
which neither dies nor can be grasped
even after countless killings,
the flames that burn it to ashes—
it turns them again into wings.
How pointless to seek deathlessness, in its body's autopsy.

क्रौंच-वध

हम एक नाज़ुक दौर से
गुज़र रहे देश की
दर्दनाक हालत हैं,
    मौत की अदालत में
    अपराधी की तरह खड़ी
    ज़िन्दगी की वकालत हैं,
नफ़रतों से भरी दुनिया में
दम तोड़ती
बेगुनाही का बयान हैं,
    जिसका ख़ून अब नसों में नहीं
    सड़कों पर बह रहा
    वो अभागे इन्सान हैं,
ज़ालिम हवाओं में
टहनी टहनी सूखता प्यार
एक घायल दरख़्त हैं,
    अपनी ही जड़ों पर
    कुल्हाड़ी चलाते आदमी का
    बहुत बुरा वक़्त हैं...

'राम राम' से 'मरा मरा' की ओर
लौटते क्या हम
दीमकों का घर हैं?
क्रौंच-वध पर
बिलख उठे अनुष्टुप् के
कदाचित हम सब से करुण स्वर हैं।

242

The Killing of the Heron[23]

We are the aching wound
of a nation passing
through fragile times,
    the defence for life
    standing like a convict
    in the courtroom of death,
We are the testament
of innocence breathing its last
in a world brimming with venom,
    the hapless, star-crossed people
    whose blood now flows
    not in veins but in streets,
A wounded tree, love
drying out twig by twig
under the merciless winds,
    we are the bad times
    of a man with an axe
    hatcheting his own roots...

Returning from *rama rama*
back to *mara mara*, are we
a home for termites to dwell in?

Perhaps, we are the most tender
note in the sloka that had bewailed
the killing of the heron then.

अनिश्चय

मुझमें फिर एक अनुपस्थिति का शोक है,
और मैं उसमें ज़िन्दा हूँ।

एक अकारण शुरुआत और अकारण मृत्यु के बीच
कहाँ हूँ?

मैं कोमल हुआ था यहीं कहीं जैसे एक फूल।
मैं कठोर हो गया हूँ जैसे मेरी यादगार का पत्थर।
जड़ता
जैसे अभी आक्रमण करेगी।

अनेक अतीतों और अनेक भविष्यों के बीच
मैंने वर्तमान को कभी-कभी ऐसे भी ठहर जाते देखा है
मानो वह केवल
स्मृतियों में जाग रहा,
एक जन्मसिद्ध समय
जीने से भाग रहा।

कितनी कठिन यातना है
इस तरह अकस्मात एक ज़िन्दा पल का ठहरे रह जाना
वहीं का वहीं। अव्यतीत। अघटित। अवाक़।
और रोज़ पैदा होते नये-नये वीरानों का चिल्लाना बेज़बान—

बीत, कुछ तो बीत हम पर
ज़िन्दगी या मौत-सा स्पष्ट,
हमको अनिश्चय से चीरते क्षण... बीत

Uncertainty

For Stephen Hawking

Again the sorrow of an absence in me
and I am alive in it.

Between a dawn without cause and a death
without reason, where am I?

    Somewhere here I became
    tender like a flower.
    I have hardened now like my tombstone.
    As if stillness
    may just assail me.

Between many pasts and many futures
I have also seen the present sometimes
pause in such a way
    as if it was only
    awake in remembrance,
    a time inborn
    scurrying away from existence.

What a terrible torment it is
for a living moment to stay paused like this, suddenly.
Right there. Unspent. Unpassed. Unspoken.
And the tongueless scream of new wildernesses born daily—

    pass, come to pass on us
    something vivid like life or death,
    moments rending us with uncertainty... pass

कैसे लोग हैं हम

उसने तो सिर्फ़ आह भरी थी
मैंने ही कुछ ज़्यादा सुना

वह थाने नहीं गई
नहीं लिखाई प्राथमिकी
उसने तो न्याय भी नहीं माँगा था

वे ही डर गये थे
उसकी चीख़ती ख़ामोशी से

वह तो अस्पताल भी नहीं गई थी
उसने ख़ुद ही सी लिया था अपना पेट
अपने ही हाथों से

उसे तो मृत घोषित कर चुके थे अख़बार

फिर कैसे बची रह गई उसमें
मृत्यु के बाद भी इतनी जान
कि धरती फाड़ कर निकल पड़ा
उसकी धमनियों से रक्त का फ़व्वारा

अब वह नहीं
सब परेशान हैं कि हम कैसे लोग हैं।
कैसा वक़्त है यह।

What People Are We [24]

she had only sighed
it is I who heard some more

she did not go to the police
nor file a complaint
nor even seek justice

it is they who got scared
of her screaming silence

she did not even go to the hospital
she stitched up her womb herself
with her own hands

she had been declared
dead by newspapers

then how is it that so much life
was left in her even after death
that a fountain of blood gushed out from her veins
ripping the earth apart...

now, she is not
but all of us are uneasy—
        what people are we
        what times are these

बुरे वक़्तों की कविता

ब्रेख़्त को याद करते हुए

कैसी हो ऐसे
बुरे वक़्तों की कविता?

कवि बदलते
कविताएँ बदलतीं
पर बदलते ही नहीं बुरे वक़्त।

बहुत-सी मुश्किलें
ढूँढ़ती हैं शब्द आसान भाषा में
चाहती हैं कि वे उठें बूँद-बूँद
भाप की तरह गहरे समुद्रों से
पहाड़ों से टकरायें बादलों की तरह
घेर कर बरसें पृथ्वी को
जैसे आँधी पानी बिजली...

और बहा ले जाए बुरे वक़्तों को
बुरे वक़्तों की कविता।

कैसे हो बुरे वक़्तों की कविता...

Poetry of Dark Times

Remembering Brecht

How should be
the poetry of dark times
like this?

Poets change, poems change,
but dark times
just don't seem to change.

So much misery
keeps looking for words in artless language,
keeps wishing that they arise
    drop by drop
    like vapour from abyssal oceans
    collide with mountains
    like nimbus clouds
    girdle the earth and rain down on it
    like tempest thunder lightning...

        and so let the poetry of dark times inundate
        and wash away the dark times.

How can the poetry
of dark times
be...

विभक्त व्यक्तित्व

मुक्तिबोध के निधन पर

वह थक कर बैठ गया जिस जगह
वह न पहली, न अन्तिम
न नीचे, न ऊपर
न यहाँ, न वहाँ...

कभी लगता—एक कदम आगे सफलता।
कभी लगता—पाँवों के आसपास जल भरता।

सोचता हूँ उससे विदा ले लूँ
वह जो बुद्ध-सा चिन्तामग्न हिलता न डुलता।
वह शायद अन्य है क्योंकि अन्यतम है।

वैसे जीना किस जीने से कम है
जबकि वह कहीं से भी अपने को लौटा ले सकता था
शिखर से साधारण तक,
शब्दों के अर्थजाल से केवल उनके उच्चारण तक।

सिद्धि के रास्ते जब दुनिया घटती
और व्यक्ति बढ़ता है,
कितनी अजीब तरह
अपने-आपसे अलग होना पड़ता है।

On the Death of Poet Muktibodh

The place where he sat down tired
was not the first nor the last
neither down nor up
not here nor there...

At times—triumph felt a step away from him.
At times—water around his feet held him.

Maybe one should bid him farewell—
he who neither moves nor stirs, like the Buddha
in contemplation. He is perhaps
an exception, as he is exceptional.

Living thus is no less a way of living
whereas he could have retreated from anywhere,
from the pinnacle to the quotidian,
from the web of meaning behind words
to only their utterance.

On the path to realisation
when the world recedes
and a person moves ahead,
how strangely one has to
part from oneself.

बहन को याद करते हुए

शायद वही है जो मेरे जीवन में
वापस आना चाहती है बार बार
  लेकिन जिसे हर बार
  बरबस बाहर कर दिया जाता है
  मेरे जीवन से

मैं जानता हूँ
वह है कहीं
  मेरे बिल्कुल पास, गुमसुम,
  मुझे घेर कर बैठी
  एक असह्य उदासी

वह नहीं मानती
  कि हमारे बीच अब
  बरसों का फ़ासला है,
  और सारे बन्धन
    कब के टूट चुके हैं

Recalling My Sister[25]

Perhaps it is she
who wishes to come back herself
again and again to my life
  but is forced out of it
  each time
  emphatically

I know that she
is there   somewhere
    very close to me,
    sitting hushed and distrait,
    surrounding me silently
        an unbearable melancholy
—doesn't accept that
between us now
there's a distance of many years
    and all bonds
    have long been undone

एक दिन जैसे एक राग

आओ शुरू करें एक दिन
जैसे एक राग

विलम्बित में
आलाप से

जैसे शुरू होती है सुबह
धीरे-धीरे

स्वरों और फिरत से बढ़त लेती
मध्य लय में ठहरती हुई
द्रुत में प्रवेश करती
तानों का सधा हुआ भराव

और अन्ततः
तराने की जटिल ऊँचाइयों को छूते हुए
धीरे-से विसर्जित हो जाँय
एक लम्बे मौन के
खिंचते समापन में

राग भटियाली

एक राग है भटियाली
बाउल संगीत से जुड़ा हुआ

अन्तिम स्वर को
खुला छोड़ दिया जाता है
वायुमण्डल में लहराता हुआ
जैसे सम्पूर्ण जीवन राग से
युक्त हुई एक ध्वनि
अनन्त में विलीन हो गई...

वह शेष स्वरों को बाँधता नहीं
इसलिए अन्त में भी
उनसे बँधता नहीं,
अन्तिम आह जैसा कुछ
एक अजीब तरह की मुक्ति का
एहसास देता है वह...

A Diptych of Ragas

For music maestro Amir Khan

A Day, A Raga

Come, let us begin
one day like a raga

In slow time,
starting with a prelude,
like a morning begins
little by little

Then, taking tempo
from tones and trills,
meandering mid-pace,
flowing into fast flight,
saturate the scales
with structured notes

And finally
coursing the complex
crests of cadence,
let us slowly be immersed
in the lingering finale
of a long silence…

Raga Bhatiyali

In Baul music
there is a raga called
Bhatiyali

Its final note
is left unlaced, swaying
in the dome of the sky
like a sound saturated
with the full raga
of life, fading into
infinity

It doesn't bind
the remaining notes
and so in the end isn't
bound by them either

Something like a last sigh
it seems to give us
a strange sense
of liberty

अमरत्व से थका आकाश

कभी कभी लगता बेहद
थक चुका है आकाश
अपनी बेहदी से

वह सीमित होना चाहता है
एक छोटी-सी गृहस्थी भर जगह में
शामिल होना चाहता है
एक पारिवारिक दिनचर्या में
प्रेमी होना चाहता है
पिता होना चाहता है
होना चाहता है किसी के आँगन की धूप

वह अविचल मौन से विचलित हो
ध्वनित और प्रतिध्वनित होना चाहता है शब्दों में
फूल फल पत्ते होना चाहते हैं उसके चाँद और तारे
आँसू होना चाहती हैं ओस की बूँदें...

अमरत्व से थक चुकी
आकाश की अटूट उबासी
अकस्मात् टूट कर
होना चाहती है
किसी मृत्यु के बाद की उदासी

A Sky Tired of Eternity

Sometimes the sky appears infinitely
weary of its own
unrelenting infinity…

It wants to shackle itself down
to the snug space of a home,
it wants to be a part
of some familial routine,
wants to be a lover,
a child's parent,
the sunlight of someone's patio

Unsettled by a standstill silence, it wants to
sound and resound in words,
its moon and stars want to become
fruits foliage flowers
drops of dew
want to become tears…

Tired of immortality,
the unbroken yawn of the sky
wants to break off all at once
and become the lament
of after some death

तुम मेरे हर तरफ़

और तुम मेरे हर तरफ़
    हर वक़्त
    इतनी मौजूद :
    मेरी दुनिया में
    तुम्हारा बराबर आना-जाना

फिर भी ठीक से पहचान में न आना
    कि कह सकूँ
    देखो, यह रही मेरी पहचान
    मेरी अपनी बिल्कुल अपनी
    सबसे पहलेवाली
    या सबसे बादवाली
    किसी भी चीज़ की तरह
    बिल्कुल स्पष्ट और निश्चित।

अब उसे चिंतित करते मेरी उँगलियों के बीच से
निचुड़कर बह जाते दृश्यों के रंग,
लोगों और चीज़ों के वर्णन
भाषा के बीच की ख़ाली जगहों में गिर जाते।

    ठहरे पानी के गहरे डुबाव में
    एक परछाईं एक परत और सिकुड़ती।
    शाम के अँधेरे ठण्डे हाथ।
    मेरे कन्धों पर बर्फ़ की तरह ठण्डे हाथ
    मुझे महसूस करते हैं।

You, All Around Me

And you, all around me
    all the time
    so present:
    in my world
    you ceaselessly come and go

And yet, you do not come in recognition
    so that I could say
    see, this is my recognition
    my own, my very own
    the very first
    or the very last
    like any other thing
    so clear and crystalline.

Now, when I paint you, the colours of vistas
are wrung out, and flow away
from between my fingers,
vignettes of people and things
fall between the empty coves of language.

    In the sinking depth of still water
    a shadow shrinks by another fold.
    The dark clammy hands of evening.

    Hands cold like ice on my shoulders
    feel me.

किसी और ने नहीं

नहीं, किसी और ने नहीं
मैंने ही तोड़ दिया है कभी कभी
अपने को झूठे वादे की तरह
यह जानते हुए भी कि बार बार
        लौटना है मुझे
        प्रेम की तरफ़
विश्वास बनाये रखना है
        मनुष्य में
सिद्ध करते रहना है
        कि मैं टूटा नहीं

        चाहे कविता बराबर ही
        जुड़े रहना है किसी तरह
        सब से।

No One Else

No, no one else,
it is I who have sometimes broken
myself like a false promise
knowing well that again and again
  I have to return
    to love
  have to keep faith
    in people
  have to keep proving
    that I have not been broken

    if only
    by as much as a poem
    I have to somehow stay linked
    to all

Notes

1. Written in the 1970s during India's 'Emergency'; Dhoomil (Sudama Panday), a contemporary poet and friend of the author, died young in a hospital.

2. At Montmartre Cemetery, Paris; the poem's first title was 'Between Two Dates'.

3. The author's contemporary and poet-friend, who was very fond of this poem.

4. The translation was first published as 'The Albatross', alluding to a sense of guilt or responsibility, as in 'an albatross around one's neck'.

5. Lucknow, 1985; in Hindi, the word *Śānti* (peace) can also be someone's name.

6. River Saryu flows through the poet's childhood town, Ayodhya; legend has it that Lord Rama, Ayodhya's king, may have ended his life by drowning himself in it.

7. Theatre person Ebrahim Alkazi directed Girish Karnad's play *Tughlaq* about Muhammad bin Tughlaq (reign 1325-51), famously staged at the Purana Qila in Delhi.

8. Golkunda, or Golconda, a fortified citadel and capital of the Deccan Sultanate of the Qutb Shahi dynasty (1518-1687), is situated near present-day Hyderabad.

9. Ghalib, Mir, Kabir, Surdas and Tulsidas, among India's greatest poets, are said to have led modest lives.

10. Bhartrihari, 6th-7th century poet-king (often seen as the philosopher-grammarian who wrote *Vākyapadīya* or *Words in a Sentence*), led a sensuous, luxurious life. Of his wives, he loved queen Pingala most. It is said that a saint once gave him a fruit 'for eternal youth'. He gave it to Pingala, but she passed it on to a stablekeeper whom she loved; he in turn gave it to another. The fruit travelled back to the king. He learnt of Pingala's betrayal and was disillusioned. Following the example of Indian sages, and after a long self-struggle, he became a yogi—living in a cave near modern-day Ujjain until his death. He is said to have written the *Śatakatraya* comprising three 'śatakas' (sets of hundred verses)—*Śriṅgāra* (love)-*śataka*, *Nīti* (ethics/polity)-*śataka*, and *Vairāgya* (dispassion)-*śataka*. Scholars confidently attribute only the first to him.

11. Vijayanagara, the now-ruined capital of the historic Vijayanagara Empire, surrounds modern-day Hampi in Karnataka. Around 1500 CE, it was one of the world's largest cities, prospering under the rule of the brothers

Hakka (Harihara I) and Bukka (Bukka Raya I) in the 14th century. 'Hakkā-Bakkā' in Hindi also means taken aback, a pun to imply that the city now stood stunned. Sayana, a Sanskrit scholar, lived in the empire; his *Rigveda* commentary was translated by Max Müller.

12. Anarkali, a legendary courtesan in the times of the Mughal emperor Akbar during the 16th century, is said to have been entombed in a wall on Akbar's orders for having a relationship with prince Salim (later Emperor Jahangir). Scholars are not agreed on the tale's authenticity. In the poem, an evening in Lahore's Bazaar Anarkali is conflated with a recollection of the incident and Salim re-living it.

13. Chandragupta Maurya (reign 321-297 BCE), founder of the Mauryan Empire and the first king to unify most of Greater India into one state, with his advisor Chanakya, gave India a glorious stature. He later abdicated his throne, embraced Jainism and became an ascetic; he died in Shravanabelagola in Karnataka.

14. Reference is to a couplet by the poet Ghalib in which a *Birahaman/Brāhmin* soothsayer predicts that the year will be good for him, and Ghalib takes this amusingly.

15. On a sketch of the author made by poet Yang Lian in Rome, 2006.

16. In Indian mythology, Sudama was a poor childhood friend of Lord Krishna (Girdhari), ruler of legendary Dwarika now sunk under the sea. Once, in difficulty, Sudama went to Krishna with the modest gift of some rice, who nevertheless hosted him generously. The poem has ironic references to a Delhi suburb 'Dwarka', to money-spinning Bollywood dances, and to the frivolity of urban consumerism.

17. A *maṁdapa* (temple hall) lies between an *ardhamaṁdapa* (entrance porch) and *mahāmaṁdapa* (great hall), leading to the *garbhagriha* (sanctum sanctorum or 'womb') via an *antarāla* (vestibule). These liminal architectural elements between the exterior and divine worlds often have erotic carvings in Khajuraho, like those of the *apsarā* (celestial nymph), *devadāsī* (female attendant of God) and *śāl bhanjikā* (sylph grasping the *śāl* tree), as also mythical creatures like the *śārdūl* (griffin).

18. The last stanza refers to the idea of *puruṣa* (the unchanging element or soul) and *prakṛti* (the changing element or nature)—and their union that makes creation possible—in *Sāṁkhya* philosophy.

19. Writer's Home alludes to Tagore's time in Ramgarh with his ailing daughter in the mountains; Naukuchiya Taal, near Ramgarh, is a lake, meaning 'nine-cornered lake'.

20. Kanakbhavan is a venerated temple in Ayodhya city; *tesū* are the bright orange 'Flame of the Forest' (Butea Monosperma) flowers associated with spring.

21. Nature's nascent beauty, as experienced by Vedic sages, is conflated here with the mythic, abstract beauty of Marisha, daughter of sage Kandu and divine nymph Pramlocha. In Indian mythology, Marisha was born of nature and nurtured by it.

22. *Caurapañcāśikā*, a poem in fifty stanzas by Kashmiri poet Bilhana (11th-12th century), depicts the secret erotic love of a poet 'love thief' and a princess. When found, the king condemns the poet to death. Descending fifty steps to the gallows, the poet recites one stanza at each step. The king is impressed and, on his minister's request, pardons the poet and consents for him to marry the princess. The original has several English translations, notably that by E. Powys Mathers. Names for the princess and poet vary: here *Vidyā* (knowledge) and *Sundar* (beautiful) are used.

23. Legend has it that Valmiki was a robber first; sages once told him that true treasure could only be found in (Lord) Rama, and brought him to realisation. But he couldn't utter this word, so they had him chant it in reverse as *Marā... Marā* (killed), something he could say, which soon became *Rāma... Rāma*. During his long penance, as he sat chanting, a termite-hill (*vālmīki* in Sanskrit) built around him. Later, after his transformation, he was once on a riverbank with a pair of herons in peaceful bliss nearby. Suddenly, a hunter shot one down. The painful wails of the other so shook up Valmiki that he uttered a curse, amazingly in *anuṣṭup* verse, a rhythm-type with eight syllables to a *pāda* (foot). He became a harbinger-poet, and this the first '*śloka*' of the *Rāmāyaṇa*, the first Sanskrit epic. The heron is also said to be a symbol in other cultures: of luck and patience in Native American tribes, purity in Japan, a path to heaven in China, a creator of light in Egypt, and a messenger of God in Greek myth. Its killing here is conflated with our abject times, and redemption alluded to in the epic it triggered.

24. In the aftermath of the Gujarat riots in India, 2002.

25. The poet's mother and sister died of tuberculosis very early in his life.

In the introduction, notes, bibliography and index, diacritical marks are used for transliterated Hindi words and for titles of books and poems (but not for names of places or people) for readers to have a sense of the pronunciation. Contrary to the convention, the first letters of all words in poem and book titles have been capitalised. Italics are used for names of books, transliterated Hindi words, quotations and emphasis.

Index of Original Titles

Titles of the short poems in the eight section breaks are given below the respective section headings

English Title	Hindi Title	Original Book
A THIRD HISTORY		
• The Hilt of a Broken Dagger	Ṭūṭe Hue Khaṁjar Kī Mūṭh	Koī Dūsrā Nahīṁ
24. An Evening in Golconda	Golkuṇḍā Kī Ek Śām	Koī Dūsrā Nahīṁ
25. Nero's Love of Music	Nīro Kā Saṁgīt-Prem	Hāśiye Kā Gavāh
26. In the Lanes and Bylanes of the Past	Atīt Ke Galī Kūcom Meṁ	Hāśiye Kā Gavāh
27. The Estrangement of Bhartṛhari	Bhartṛhari Kī Virakti	Hāśiye Kā Gavāh
28. Vijaynagar, The City of Victory	Vijayanagara	Koī Dūsrā Nahīṁ
29. Bazaar Anarkali, Lahore—A Twilight	'Bāzār Anārkalī', Lāhaur—Ek Śām	Hāśiye Kā Gavāh
30. Those Who Do Not Know	Ve Jo Nahīṁ Jānte	Hāśiye Kā Gavāh
31. The Last Days of Chandragupta Maurya	Caṁdragupta Maurya	In Dinoṁ
I REACHED THE WORLD A LITTLE LATE		
• A Better World	(Untitled)	Sab Itnā Asamāpt
32. Hesitation	Asmaṁjas	Hāśiye Kā Gavāh
33. A Little Late in This World	Zarā Der Se Is Duniyā Meṁ	Sab Itnā Asamāpt
34. Arrival of the Barbarians	Barbarom Kā Āgaman	Apne Sāmne
35. A World Under My Feet	Phir Mere Pāṁvoṁ Tale	In Dinoṁ
36. Mega Truth	Mahāsac	In Dinoṁ
37. The Pandemic of Numbers	Āṁkaṛoṁ Kī Bīmārī	Koī Dūsrā Nahīṁ
38. Horoscope for the Year	Varṣphal	Hāśiye Kā Gavāh
39. Belle in the Coffin	Tābūt Kī Sundarī	Sab Itnā Asamāpt
40. Horsemen	Ghuṛsavār	Hāśiye Kā Gavāh
41. God Is Our Witness	Īśvar Sākṣī Hai	Sab Itnā Asamāpt
42. The Happier I Wish to Keep Them	Jitnā Hī Khuś Rakhnā Cāhtā Hūṁ	Sab Itnā Asamāpt
43. Words that Disappear	Śabd Jo Kho Jāte Haiṁ	Sab Itnā Asamāpt
OF ANOTHER TIME, ANOTHER PLACE		
• Gypsy Heart	Baṁjārā Man	Hāśiye Kā Gavāh
44. Angkor Wat	Aṁkor Vaṭ	Sab Itnā Asamāpt
45. With Nazim Hikmet, 1955	Nāzim Hikmat Ke Sāth, 1955	Hāśiye Kā Gavāh
46. Meeting Pablo Neruda, Warsaw 1955	Pāblo Nerudā Se Ek Bheṁṭ, Vārsā 1955	Hāśiye Kā Gavāh
47. A Well in Tunisia	Tyūnīśiā Kā Kuāṁ	Hāśiye Kā Gavāh
48. Contemplating a Sketch of Me Made by a Chinese Poet-Friend	Ek Cīnī Kavimitra Dvārā Banāye Apne Ek Rekhācitra Ko Socte Hue	Hāśiye Kā Gavāh
49. Historic Separations	Aitihāsik Fāsle	Hāśiye Kā Gavāh
50. Sudama in Dwarika	Dvārikā Meṁ Sudāmā	Hāśiye Kā Gavāh
51. Qutab Minar	Qutubmīnār	Apne Sāmne
52. Khajuraho	Khajurāho	In Dinoṁ
53. Some Days in Another Time, Another Place	Kuch Din Anya Deśkāl Meṁ	In Dinoṁ

English Title	Hindi Title	Original Book
THE WISH OF A LEAF		
• In the Park	*Pārk Meṁ*	*Hāśiye Kā Gavāh*
54. Invitation	*Ātithya*	*Sab Itnā Asamāpt*
55. Ramgarh Triptych	*Rāmgaṛh*	*Hāśiye Kā Gavāh*
• Quiet Space	• *Śānta Sthalī*	
• Writer's Home	• *Rāitars Hom*	
• Naukuchiya Taal	• *Naukuciyā Tāl*	
56. Unbroken	*Aṭūṭ Hissā*	*Koī Dūsrā Nahīṁ*
57. The Rainforests of Namdapha	*Namdāphā Ke Varṣā-Van*	*Hāśiye Kā Gavāh*
58. Next to a Paved Road	*Pakkī Saṛak Ke Kināre*	*Koī Dūsrā Nahīṁ*
59. Wild Rose	*Jaṁglī Gulāb*	*Sab Itnā Asamāpt*
60. Colours of Melancholy	*Udāsī Ke Raṁg*	*Hāśiye Kā Gavāh*
61. Sunayana	*Sunayanā*	*Koī Dūsrā Nahīṁ*
62. A Sparrow's Song	*Gauraiyā*	*Sab Itnā Asamāpt*
63. The Book of the Forest	*Jaṁgal Kī Kitāb*	*Sab Itnā Asamāpt*
64. The Thirst of Water	*Pānī Kī Pyās*	*In Dinoṁ*
THE MYRIAD LANGUAGES OF LOVE		
• So Much in the World	*Itnā Kuch Thā Duniyā Meṁ*	*Hāśiye Kā Gavāh*
65. Marisha	*Māriṣā*	*Hāśiye Kā Gavāh*
66. First Light	*Ujās*	*Hāśiye Kā Gavāh*
67. Chaur Panchashika: Even Today	*Adyāpi*	*Koī Dūsrā Nahīṁ*
68. The Languages of Love	*Pyār Kī Bhāṣāē*	*Hāśiye Kā Gavāh*
69. Being Nature	*Nisarga*	*Sab Itnā Asamāpt*
70. Before Getting Drenched in the Rain	*Bāriś Meṁ Bhīgane Se Pahle*	*Hāśiye Kā Gavāh*
71. Telimena	*Telīmenā*	*Sab Itnā Asamāpt*
72. New-Found Books	*Naī Kitābeṁ*	*Hāśiye Kā Gavāh*
73. Poetry: 1 & 2	*Kavitā & Kavitā Kī Zarūrat*	*Koī Dūsrā Nahīṁ*
74. A Twilight Stroll	*Śām Kī Sair*	*Hāśiye Kā Gavāh*
75. Nearness	*Nikaṭṭā*	*Sab Itnā Asamāpt*
76. Postscript: So Close to Me	*Mere Itne Pās*	*Sab Itnā Asamāpt*
PASS, SOMETHING PASS US BY		
• To That Pain	*Us Dard Ko*	*Sab Itnā Asamāpt*
77. Words Too Are Left Behind	*Śabd Tak*	*Sab Itnā Asamāpt*
78. Post-Mortem of a Phoenix	*Śav-Parīkṣā*	*Koī Dūsrā Nahīṁ*
79. The Killing of the Heron	*Krauṁca-Vadha*	*Koī Dūsrā Nahīṁ*
80. Uncertainty	*Aniścaya*	*Apne Sāmne*
81. What People Are We	*Kaise Log Haiṁ Ham*	*Hāśiye Kā Gavāh*
82. Poetry of Dark Times	*Bure Vaqtoṁ Kī Kavitā*	*Sab Itnā Asamāpt*
83. On the Death of Poet Muktibodh	*Vibhakta Vyaktitva*	*Apne Sāmne*
84. Recalling My Sister	*Bahan Ko Yād Karte Hue*	*Sab Itnā Asamāpt*
85. A Diptych of Ragas		
• A Day, A Raga	• *Ek Din Jaise Ek Rāga*	*In Dinoṁ*
• Raga Bhatiyali	• *Rāga Bhatiyālī*	*Sab Itnā Asamāpt*
86. A Sky Tired of Eternity	*Amratva Se Thakā Ākāś*	*Sab Itnā Asamāpt*
87. You, All Around Me	*Tum Mere Har Taraf*	*Apne Sāmne*
88. No One Else	*Kisī Aur Ne Nahīṁ*	*Koī Dūsrā Nahīṁ*

Kunwar Narain: Selected Bibliography

With approximate English translations of Hindi titles

Poetry

Cakravyūh (Circular Siege), 1956, Radhakrishan Prakashan, Delhi
Tīsrā Saptak (Third Heptad), ed. Agyeya, 1959, Jnanpith Prakashan, Delhi
Pariveś : Ham-Tum (Surroundings: Us-You), 1961, Vani Prakashan, Delhi
Apne Sāmne (In Front of Us), 1979, Rajkamal Prakashan, Delhi*
Koī Dūsrā Nahīṁ (No One the Other), 1993, Rajkamal Prakashan, Delhi*
In Dinoṁ (These Days), 2002, Rajkamal Prakashan, Delhi* ·
Hāśiye Kā Gavāh (Witness in the Margin), 2009, Medha Books, Delhi*
Sab Itnā Asamāpt (All So Unfinished), 2018, Rajkamal Prakashan, Delhi*

Epical Poems

Ātmajayī (Self-Conqueror), based on the Upanishadic episode of Naciketa, 1965, Jnanpith Prakashan, Delhi
Vājaśravā Ke Bahāne (On Vajashrava's Pretext), recalling the memory of Ātmajayī from forty years ago, 2008, Jnanpith Prakashan, Delhi
Kumārajīva, based on the life and times of the Buddhist scholar-translator Kumarajiva, 2015, Jnanpith Prakashan, Delhi

Short Stories

Ākāroṁ Ke Ās-Pās (Near and Around Shapes), 1971, Radhakrishan, Delhi
Bécain Pattoṁ Kā Koras (The Chorus of Restless Leaves), ed. Amrendra Nath Tripathi, 2018, Rajkamal Prakashan, Delhi

Literary Criticism

Āj Aur Āj Se Pahle (Today and Before Today), 1998, Rajkamal Prakashan, Delhi
Sāhitya Ke Kuch Antar-Viṣayak Sandarbh (Some Interdisciplinary Contexts of Literature), XIV Samvatsar Lecture, 2003, Sahitya Akademi
Rukh (Stance), ed. Anurag Vats, 2014, Rajkamal Prakashan, Delhi

Other Non-Fiction

Diśāoṁ Kā Khulā Ākāś (An Open Sky of Many Ways), jottings, ed. Yatindra Mishra, 2012, Vani Prakashan, Delhi
Śabd Aur Deśkāl (Words and Space-Time), essays, 2013, Rajkamal, Delhi
Lekhak Kā Sinemā (A Writer's Cinema), Narain's writings on world cinema, ed. Geet Chaturvedi, 2017, Rajkamal Prakashan, Delhi

---

* The poems in *Witnesses of Remembrance* have been selected from these collections.

Conversations

Mere Sākṣātkār, interviews given by Kunwar Narain, ed. Vinod Bhardwaj, 1999, updated edition, 2010, Kitabghar Prakashan, Delhi

Taṭ Par Hūṁ Par Taṭastha Nahīṁ, Kunwar Narain's conversations, ed. Vinod Bhardwaj, 2010, Rajkamal Prakashan, Delhi

Jiye Hue Se Zyādā: Kūvar Nārāyaṇ Ke Sāth Saṁvād, conversations with Kunwar Narain, 2023, Rajkamal Prakashan, Delhi

Translations of World Poetry

Selected poems of Constantine Cavafy & Jorge Luis Borges, *Tanāv*, 1986 & 1987

Poems of Tadeusz Różewicz in *W Środku Życia* & Zbigniew Herbert in *Obszar Pamięci*, eds. Ashok Vajpeyi & Renata Czekalska, 2001 & 2003, Vani Prakashan

Na Sīmāẽ Na Dūriyāṁ (No Limits No Distances), Kunwar Narain's translations of 30 European and world poets, 2017, Vani Prakashan, Delhi

Selections and Compilations

Kūvar Nārāyaṇ: Saṁsār-I (World: Selected Writings of Kunwar Narain), ed. Y Mishra, 2002, Vani Prakashan, Delhi

Kūvar Nārāyaṇ: Upasthiti-II (Presence: Selected Writings on Kunwar Narain's work), ed. Y Mishra, 2002, Vani Prakashan, Delhi

Kūvar Nārāyaṇ: Cunī Huī Kavitāẽ (Selected Poems), ed. S Salil, 2007, Medha, Delhi

Kūvar Nārāyaṇ: Pratinidhi Kavitāẽ (Representative Poems), ed. Purushottam Agarwal, 2008, Rajkamal Prakashan, Delhi

Kunwar Narain: No Other World: Selected Poems, translated by Apurva Narain, 2008, Rupa Publications, Delhi & 2010, Arc Publications, UK

Kūvar Nārāyaṇ: Pacās Kavitāẽ (Fifty Poems), 2011, Vani Prakashan, Delhi

Kūvar Nārāyaṇ: Kaī Samayoṁ Meṁ (Kunwar Narain: In Many Times), eds. DK Shukla & Y Misra, 2012, Jnanpith Prakashan, Delhi

Kunwar Narain: Kavi Svar / The Poet's Voice, Vols. I & II, selected poems in the poet's voice, Sadho Recitations, 2013, Delhi

Kūvar Nārāyaṇ: Kavi Né Kahā (Kunwar Narain: The Poet Said), selected poems, 2014, Kitabghar Prakashan, Delhi

Jīne Kā Udātta Āśaya, Sandarbha: Kūvar Nārāyaṇ Kī Kavitā (The Sublime Intention of Living: Kunwar Narain's Poetry), literary criticism, Pankaj Chaturvedi, 2015, Rajkamal Prakashan, Delhi

Anvaya–I: Sāhitya Ke Parisar Meṁ Kūvar Nārāyaṇ, Writings on Kunwar Narain's overall work, ed. Om Nischal, 2018, Rajkamal Prakashan, Delhi

Anviti–II: Sāhitya Ke Parisar Meṁ Kūvar Nārāyaṇ, Writings on Narain's specific works, ed. Om Nischal, 2018, Rajkamal Prakashan, Delhi

Kunwar Narain: The Play of Dolls: Stories, translated by John Vater & Apurva Narain, 2020, Penguin Modern Classics, Penguin Books, India

Narain's work has been translated into some 35 languages so far, with book-length translations in English, Italian, Polish, Estonian, Russian, Spanish, Marathi, Odiya, Assamese, Dogri, Gujarati, Punjabi and Kannada (forthcoming in French, Bulgarian and Malayalam). There are books and theses on his work, and films on his poems. His work has appeared in anthologies and journals in Hindi and other languages, including English-language journals such as *Poetry, MPT, TriQuarterly, Asymptote, Chicago Review, The Little Magazine, Manoa, Poetry International, Agenda, Pratik, The Beacon, Interim, Ploughshares, Two Lines,* etc.

Some English-language anthologies with his work include *Modern Hindi Poetry: An Anthology* (ed. Vidya N. Misra, 1965, Indiana University Press), *The Golden Waist Chain: Modern Hindi Short Stories,* (ed. Sara Rai, 1990, Penguin), *Periplus: Poetry in Translation* (eds. Daniel Weissbort & Arvind Krishna Mehrotra, 1993, Oxford University Press), *The Penguin New Writing in India* (eds. Aditya Behl & David Nicholls, 1994, Penguin), *Survival* (eds. Daniel Weissbort & Girdhar Rathi, 1994, Sahitya Akademi), *The Oxford Anthology of Modern Indian Poetry* (eds. Vinay Dharwadker & A.K. Ramanujan, 1994, Oxford University Press), *Yatra: Writings from The Indian Subcontinent* (gen. ed. Alok Bhalla, eds. Nirmal Verma & U.R. Ananthamurthy, 1994, Indus), *An Anthology of Modern Hindi Poetry* (ed. Kailash Vajpeyi, 1998, Rupa), *New Poetry in Hindi* (ed. Lucy Rosenstein, 2003, Permanent Black), *Cracow Indological Studies* (eds. Renata Czekalska & Halina Marlewicz, 2005, Jagiellonian University), *A Poem for CRY: Favourite Poems of Famous Indians* (eds. Avanti Maluste & Sudeep Doshi, 2006, Penguin Viking), *The Golden Boat: River Poems* (ed. K Satchidanandan, 2011, Yoda Press & IIC), *These My Words: The Penguin Book of Indian Poetry* (eds. Eunice De Souza & Melanie Silgardo, 2012, Penguin) and *100 Great Indian Poems* (ed. Abhay K, 2018, Bloomsbury). Journals with recent issues focusing on Narain include *Pūrvagraha (nos. 124 & 146), Hindi: Language, Discourse, Writing (Jan-Mar 2009), Samaya Mīmāṁsā (Jul-Dec 2017), Nayā Jñānodaya (Dec 2017), Hans (Jan 2018), Indraprastha Bhāratī (Sep-Oct 2018), Ājkal (Sep 2018), Chandrabhāgā (no. 19), Indian Literature (nos. 248, 305 & 308),* etc.

Scan QR code to access the
Penguin Random House India website